TH
PROTESTORS
HANDBOOK

D1628214

"This book will help you move the world in a better direction. If you want ideas for a winning strategy or inspiration for how to get involved then this is the handbook for you."

John Sauven, executive director Greenpeace UK

"For anyone wanting to do more than just complain about the state of the world, this handbook is a must-have guide to taking action. Whether it is cruelty to animals or nuclear weapons that you feel passionate about, there are plenty of ideas and inspiration for both novice and veteran activists. A book that will get you on your feet rather than curled up on the sofa!"

Dr Caroline Lucas, Green Party MEP for south-east England

"There are plenty of things not to like. From the abuses of the banking sector to climate change and from the rising power of the supermarkets to the creeping cynicism that now infects politics. This book reminds us of a very important fact, however – and that is how the power to change things is really down to us. If we sit back and moan things will probably get worse. Getting stuck in with the process of change can by contrast help bring about positive improvements. Read this book to find out how."

Tony Juniper, campaigner, writer, adviser and commentator

9030 00000 9301 0

THE PROTESTOR'S HANDBOOK

BIBI VAN DER ZEE

Legal research provided by Susanna Rickard
and Ben Silverstone

guardianbooks

LONDON BOROUGH OF WANDSWORTH

9030 00000 9301 0	
Askews	22-Apr-2010
322.4 ZEE	£7.99
	WWX0006221/0035

Published by Guardian Books 2010

2 4 6 8 10 9 7 5 3 1

Copyright © Bibi van der Zee 2008

Bibi van der Zee has asserted her right under the Copyright, Designs and Patents Act 1988 to be identified as the author of this work

This book is sold subject to the condition that it shall not, by way of trade or otherwise, be lent, resold, hired out, or otherwise circulated without the publisher's prior consent in any form of binding or cover other than that in which it is published and without a similar condition, including this condition, being imposed on the subsequent purchaser.

First published by Guardian Books in 2008 under the title *Rebel, Rebel – The protestor's handbook*

Guardian Books
Kings Place, 90 York Way
London N1 9GU

www.guardianbooks.co.uk

A CIP catalogue record for this book is available from the British Library

ISBN 978-0-85265-211-4

Typeset by Palimpsest Book Production Limited, Grangemouth, Stirlingshire

Printed and bound in Great Britain by CPI Bookmarque Ltd, Croydon, Surrey

Contents

Acknowledgments

Many thanks to:
Susanna Rickard and Ben Silverstone for so much hard work and
extensive legal research. Paul Reynolds for his help with legal
research, in particular in pointing out aspects of Northern Irish law.
Martin Soames gave useful legal advice, as did Sean Humber. Richard
Thompson of Doughty Street Chambers was also very helpful. Phil
McLeish, who read the chapter on legal action. William Moy, who
made useful suggestions for the chapter on lobbying. James
MacKenzie for his help with lobbying and going into politics. Diana
Mackie and Caroline Howe at the Institute of Fundraising for help
with fundraising. Tracey Jennings at FMCM for her help with media.
Albert Beale, editor of the Peace Diary, for help with the contacts
list. Eric Hilaire for help with pictures. Becky Lewis and Amelia
Hodsdon for their help with the phone book. Index on Censorship
and Ctrl.Alt.Shift for allowing me to reprint work originally published
by them. Eric Gordon, Felicity Lawrence, Lesley Plommer, John
Vidal, Leo Hickman, Alison Benjamin and Jessica Aldred. Professor
Matthew Grenby, Matthew Herbert, Kathryn Tulip, Mark Thomas,
Milan Rai, Mark Farmaner, Lisa Johnson, Judith Whateley, Julie
Alexander, Billy Bragg, Ron Bailey, Dave Boyle, James Savage, Joe
Zacune, Gabriel Carlyle, Jason Torrance, Rebecca Lush Blum, Oliver
Burkeman, Emma Del Torto, Robbie the Pict, Christabel Gurney,
Ian Scoones, Benedict Southworth, Iain Scollay, Jenny Kleeman and
Frances Wright. You'll probably all disagree with me. My editor,
Phil Daoust, and my publisher, Lisa Darnell, who both made the
book happen. Sam, Ben and Joe for being no help at all but making

me smile. Emma, Jane, Jenny and Patricia, Joanna Jeffcoat, Mama and Papa, Eve, Andy and Howie. And most of all, Mike. Thank you.

Introduction

I began this book because the idea of campaigning, of protesting, of raising your voice on behalf of others, gives me profound pleasure somewhere in my middle. There are millions of people around the world today who are taking matters into their own hands, and they are continuing the work of others before them who have fought for the right to make their own decisions, to own their own land, to refuse to wage war, or just to paint their house an unusual shade of pink. It is a view of our history, an aspect of our society, that I find infinitely preferable to others. There should be much more of it.

Far too many of us, however, have no idea how easy it is to get up and do something. "Isn't that illegal?" has been the response to some of the tactics I've looked at in this book. "Not if you do it in a legal way" is the answer (although some tactics are deliberately illegal – that is the actual tactic itself). If you want to get into a corporation's annual general meeting, for example, you don't have to break into the venue and camp in the kitchen overnight: you can just buy a share in the company, which legally entitles you to be present. Other options, such as letter-writing and lobbying, are far simpler and more effective than you might imagine.

So this is my attempt to make the weapons of campaigning as accessible as possible. I've spoken to campaigners from the right, left and centre to find the simplest and most effective ways of using these weapons. I've sought mainly legal ways of taking action, and, with the indispensable aid of the legal researchers Susanna Rickard and

Ben Silverstone, set out our rights and the laws that circumscribe them in areas such as marches, demonstrations, protest camps and everything else we could think of.

These weapons need to be used. After it took so many centuries, so much blood, so much anger and pain and disappointment for ordinary men and women to win the vote, and at least a measure of equality, we seem to have surrendered our self-determination without even thinking about it. A powerful group of multinational corporations, and international financial and political institutions such as the World Bank, the International Monetary Fund, the European Commission, the United Nations and the World Trade Organisation, now control our lives. In many ways we are still in the powerless position of any medieval peasant: these behemoths run the world, and we have little say in their composition and their plans, and few ways of holding them accountable for their actions. The channels through which we can funnel our concerns are narrow, and usually controlled by those who have most to lose from any challenge to the status quo. All that effort, all those years spent storming parliament, and now the seat of power has moved.

There are other problems that society needs to deal with, both here in Britain and around the world. Climate change is the overwhelming issue, and it is vital to use every means to hand to push reluctant politicians into action. Write letters, picket, march – whatever you feel like this week. The more pressure we apply the better. Then there is the state's creeping intrusion into our private lives, the furious, never-ending debate about immigration, the clash of Islamism and the west. You are unlikely to be the person who can single-handedly resolve any of these issues. But your contribution may be critical. It takes a surprisingly small number of letters to persuade a politician to act, a surprisingly tiny number of complaints to persuade a company to change its policy.

Fortunately, as this book demonstrates, there are many dedicated people who are putting their hearts and souls into trying to negotiate a slightly fairer deal for everyone. The 20th century saw a huge boom in NGOs (non-governmental organisations), or "public interest groups", or "pressure groups", as they're also known: these now account for more than 4 per cent of the world's working population. A few of these organisations seem to spend their time having meetings, and their money on one pointless mail-out or television advertisement after another, but the best are astonishingly good at what they do: keeping unremitting pressure on governments and companies, and getting the issues in front of the public week after week.

But I'm even more interested in the ones who don't get paid, who far outnumber the professionals. I've come to think that politics is at its best when energetically argued by amateurs, and I've really written this book for them. The professionals, the MPs and lobbyists do not, on the whole, cast much of a glow, but the amateurs are wonderful! You would not believe the buzz at meetings that are called by volunteers and attended by volunteers, with no one being paid a penny and everyone coming just because they care. (And, OK, sometimes because there is free tea and biscuits. But the biscuits are usually pretty low-standard.) Many of the best campaigning ideas seem to come from volunteers; the passion to improve the world (in your own eyes, at least) runs very deeply indeed. In The Vote, Paul Foot's book about British democracy, a young suffragette, Charlotte Despard, encapsulates how inspiring and transformative this can be: "For me and many other young women like me, militant suffrage was the very salt of life. The knowledge of it had come like a draught of fresh air into our padded, stifled lives. It gave us release of energy, it gave us that sense of being some use in the scheme of things, without which no human being can live in peace. It made us feel that we were part of life, not just watching it ... "

The whole point of this stuff is Doing It For Yourself. It is quite remarkable what we can all do, and the sense of achievement in doing something such as organising a meeting, getting a response from a politician, setting up your own website, is – to use a horrendous but useful 60s word – empowering. I've always gone on marches, and signed petitions, and made sure that I voted. Although it seems only a small step to start organising for yourself, it is quite a difficult step: one's mind immediately silts up with worries about time, and it has to be said that this stuff tends to eat up time even faster than it eats stamps. But the compensation is that it does work. Throughout human history the people have affected the decisions of the leaders, through stone-throwing or marches or petitions, in a way that one historian described perfectly as "collective bargaining by riot". Slowly, slowly, like scarab beetles rolling dung balls up a hill, we have tried to nudge history along in the direction we want it to go. This book is a nudge to encourage nudging.

Chapter One
Why do we protest?

What would human life be like without society? In 1651, in the furnace of the English civil war, the philosopher Thomas Hobbes set out a dark vision of man as a creature in perpetual motion, driven by appetites and aversions, and always seeking to increase his power over other men, in some cases to a limitless degree. If this creature lived without controls, Hobbes argued, then it would be "warre of every man against every man" with "continuall feare, and danger of violent death; And the life of man, solitary, poore, nasty, brutish, and short." Hobbes's vision plays back still in the post-Darwinian age of Richard Dawkins, who argues that we are "survival machines – robot vehicles blindly programmed to preserve the selfish molecules known as genes".

If this is all that we are, how is it then that we cohere, how is it that we help each other and construct whole complex societies? Hobbes, again, proposed an answer: humans should "conferre all their power and strength upon one Man, or upon one Assembly of men ... and therein ... submit their Wills, every one to his Will, and their Judgements, to his Judgment ... as if every man should say to every man 'I authorise and give up my Right of Governing my selfe, to this Man, or to this Assembly of men, on this condition, that thou give up thy Right to him and Authorise all his Actions in like manner'". His personal conception of the "social contract", as it came to be known, was of an authoritarian society where all the power and rights of the subjects were ceded to an autocratic leader. Subsequent political philosophers saw that a social contract might not mean subjugation for its subjects: John Locke wanted the social contract to signify that legitimate government could exist only with the consent of the subjects, while Jean-Jacques Rousseau believed that it could create true freedom as men submitted to the rule of the general will of the people, instead of the rule of a dictator. "What man loses by the social contract," he wrote, "is his natural liberty and the absolute right to anything that tempts him and that he can take; what he gains by the social contract is civil liberty and the legal right of property in what he possesses … We might also add that man acquires with civil society, moral freedom, which alone makes man the master of himself; for to be governed by appetite alone is slavery, while obedience to a law one prescribes to oneself is freedom."

If you run a huge business, if you're the prime minister's old school-mate, if you're an international celebrity, then you may have other methods available; for most of us, however, campaigning is it. So, for example, the poll tax riots erupt in the UK in 1990 at the imposition of a levy that is widely perceived to be undemocratic and unfair. Or the people of Ukraine rise up in the Orange Revolution after crooked elections return Viktor Yanukovych, instead of the mysteriously poisoned Viktor Yushchenko. Or in 2003 millions around the world protest against an invasion of Iraq that is believed to be a cover-up for an oil and power grab. If things are not running the way we believe they should be, if we feel that our government has seriously violated the social contract, then protest is the way in which we express our displeasure.

What are the terms of this mysterious contract? Some countries set them out centuries ago, almost as soon as they had thrown off their monarchs or imperial rulers: America in its Constitution and Bill of Rights, France in the Declaration of the Rights of Man. In Britain, however, they are largely just assumed. The historian Christopher Hill records in The Century of Revolution an exchange in the House of Commons in 1641 as the MPs were in the process of impeaching King Charles I's right-hand man Lord Strafford for subverting the fundamental laws of the kingdom – a huge, rocking challenge to the King's authority. At a certain moment "the witty and malicious Edmund Waller rose, and with seeming innocence asked what the fundamental laws of the kingdom were. There was an uneasy silence. No one dared to attempt a definition which would certainly have divided the heterogenous majority ... The situation was saved by a lawyer who leapt to his feet to say that if Mr Waller did not know what the fundamental laws of the kingdom were, he had no business to be sitting in the house."

Why I fight

Joss Garman
Environmental activist

I kind of modelled my childhood on Gerald Durrell, I had a bit of a menagerie, but as I got older I moved from wanting to keep animals to wanting to protect them. When I was fourteen I started to volunteer for Greenpeace, handing anti-GM leaflets out outside Sainsbury's, writing to MPs, all that boring stuff that needs to be done. But Greenpeace don't allow anyone under 18 to get involved in direct action and more and more I was realising that direct action is what really works.

A couple of weeks after my sixteenth birthday, in the summer of 2001, I broke into Faslane naval base, and within a few days I'd been arrested three times. I was really nervous at the time, although looking back now, when I seem to be involved in direct action all the time, it's hard to remember one particular action. I was the youngest, so I suppose I wanted to prove myself, but everyone with me had been arrested before and they weren't really worried about it, so I think that rubbed off. A couple of years later I was arrested at Fairford airbase when some of us got onto the runway and tried to stop bombers taking off for Baghdad. The next day, when I was still in the cell, the papers came in with photographs of the damage those bombers had done. That made a huge impact on me. On top of that the courts were saying I might not get let out this time, and my A-levels were in a couple of weeks. That was really stressful.

Now I'm concentrating on targeting the aviation industry. I've just set up a website that will hopefully be a focal point for all the campaigns that are getting going around the country. A couple of years ago a group of us invaded an aviation industry conference – we tied rape alarms to helium balloons and let them loose in the conference hall so no one could hear a thing. We've got all sorts of people involved in the campaign to stop airport expansions – a local headmistress, a former bank manager – and I've got a really positive feeling that we can actually do this, which I don't normally get when I'm campaigning. We've only got a few years to stop Heathrow. I really think we might be able to do it.

Remarkably little has changed since then, despite the civil war or the "glorious revolution" of 1688. I think this inertia partly comes from a long-standing belief that to be British means to be free, which is built into much of our cultural life and into our self-image as the "land of hope and glory, fortress of the free". (It's possible that this belief may often mislead us about how free we really are.) Gordon Brown is talking about replacing the current mish-mash of common and statutory law with a bill of rights and responsibilities, and you can safely expect a huge amount of protesting, lobbying and campaigning if such a thing is ever written – not just about the terms of the bill, but about whether we even need such an un-British invention in the first place.

And the list of rights won since Hobbes first described his vision is quite extraordinary. Your peasant, your serf, eking out a living in the muddy fields of ancient Britain would have cackled hysterically at the idea that he or she might have the right to a vote, free health care, free education, free legal aid, social housing, unemployment benefits, sickness benefits, maternity leave, paternity leave, paid holidays … Our society would be unrecognisable to that peasant, and for many of the poorest and most disenfranchised in the world today it is probably still hardly conceivable that the citizens of western democracies enjoy such rights without falling on their knees every morning and weeping with gratitude. None of it would exist without the campaigners and protestors who have pushed and pulled along the way. The abolitionists and the labour organisers and the suffragettes have fought long, hard battles, sometimes over centuries, using every weapon to hand, from polite petitions to window-smashing and hunger strikes.

Why I fight

David Maidment
Campaigner for street children

It was 1993 and I got lost in Bombay. I found myself at Churchgate station, and because I'd always been a railway man I thought I'd be able to find my way from the train station. So I went in and was looking for someone who could give me directions when this little girl came up to me – she couldn't have been older than six or eight – and she was whipping herself. It was just so unexpected. I couldn't understand why she was doing it. It completely undid me. I couldn't cope, and I fled.

Then I pulled myself together and walked back, but by then she'd disappeared into the rush-hour crowd. I just couldn't get her out of my head, and I can still see her eyes – they were old and sort of dead. When I got back to the UK I started trying to find out about street children and realised that there was no one really trying to intercept runaway kids as they arrived at railway stations into cities. We worked out that it only took on average 20 minutes for someone – a pimp, a drug dealer, a paedophile – to pick up a child arriving alone. And I know, from my days as a railwayman, that some of these stations are not good places for children to be. If you don't get to children quickly, before they've been on the street for a while, before the drugs and all that, it's much harder to get them back to their family, or to help them.

We set up a consortium of about 25 charities, and Railway Children came about through that. About 50 per cent of our work is in India and at the moment we're running models in Russia: about 500 children a month come through the big stations in Moscow. I've seen some terrible things through this work. The first year shocked me rigid. But when I go to India now, to some of the projects we've set up and the children come running out, I see the ones who have been rescued, not the ones waiting to be rescued. If you lay awake thinking about all the others, you wouldn't be able to cope.

We're not really even halfway there, and that's the other reason why we protest. The rights may have been won, in name, but have they been implemented? In the UK, for example, article eight of the 1998 Human Rights Act states that we all have the "right to respect for his private and family life, his home and his correspondence". Yet in January 2008 it emerged that nearly 800 public bodies were making up to 1,000 requests a day to tap our phones, intercept our messages, see our bills. The United Nations agreements – the Universal Declaration of Human Rights, the Covenant on Civil and Political Rights, the Covenant on Economic, Social and Cultural Rights and so on – are seen, by some, as fairy tales, impossible to implement or work by. Global business is wresting control from the governments. The ice caps are melting. No one seems to be accountable. There's still a lot to do. The rest of this book is about how to start doing it.

Chapter Two
Coming up with a strategy

All right. You've been fulminating against the application to dig a uranium mine in your back garden for weeks now. If you're positive that no one else is doing anything about it – in which case please join them rather than confuse everyone by setting up in competition – you are now going to have to establish a campaign of your own. And, I'm afraid, all campaigns begin with a meeting.

That sounds easy enough: ring a few like-minded people, book a space or offer your front room, stick up a few posters and wait for everyone to turn up. But this meeting, the first of your campaign, is absolutely vital.

It will set the tone for everything that is to follow: if it is crisply and efficiently chaired, and ends with everyone feeling that they have a plan, that they know what they're supposed to be doing for the next week, and when you're all due to meet again, then you will end up with the beginnings of a strategy and you will have set your campaign in motion. If, however, the meeting is a fuzzy mess, with everyone disagreeing and talking over each other, if you spend the whole meeting arguing about the degeneration of solidarity, or one particularly irritating bloke is allowed to take over and hold forth about his anti-war heroics in 1982, if the meeting breaks up after two hours because people need to sort out babysitters, and you're all going to phone each other about when you'll meet up again – then you're done for. The people who actually want to achieve something won't bother to turn up next time.

The best meetings I've been to are those run by a group called

Seeds for Change, a brilliant organisation that offers training for grass-roots groups and provides expert facilitators. You may flinch at the word facilitate – but in Seeds' terms a facilitator replaces a chairman, without the despotic powers. No matter how horizontally you want to be organised, you still need someone to keep meetings moving along, and any meeting run by Seeds for Change moves along like butter. (Partly because, as one of the members says, they hate meetings so much.) And its techniques work whether you're planning to take over a power station and paint flowers on it, or send a lot of letters to everyone you can think of about the state of the hedges in the neighbourhood. You'll find contact information for Seeds for Change and many other useful organisations at the back of this book.

So, begin with a little bit of forward planning. Rather than just turning up and seeing what happens, persuade one person to facilitate the meeting, and then think it through with them very carefully. You'll need to write up an agenda, and make up a contact list, or print out contact slips. For your first meeting, you need to know what, exactly, you are campaigning about, who you are trying to reach, how you want to reach them, and how you are going to go about doing that. For some parts of the meeting you may want to break up into smaller groups for discussion: you also need to set aside time for questions, etc. If you've decided all this in advance, you will save untold hours of agonising discussion.

As far as the choice of facilitator goes, you need someone who will be firm and brisk and won't try to guide the meeting towards the conclusion that they personally favour. Someone who won't feel embarrassed about cutting someone off when they've been talking for 10 minutes, but equally won't go on an almighty power trip and take over the meeting. They need to keep things moving, to make sure that any discussion sticks to strict time limits. You can try doing it yourself, but that does mean remaining more neutral than you might always like. Perhaps it's for this reason that Seeds for Change suggests rotating the job of facilitator, so that everyone learns the necessary skills and you don't end up with a de facto leader.

It's also worth thinking about how you want decisions to be taken – on a show of hands, a secret ballot, etc. One of the anarchist techniques that has emerged from a couple of decades of direct action is consensus, which basically means you only do something when you all agree. Not just a majority, but everyone. That may seem completely impossible, but it's the way that a handful of societies run themselves. The Iroquois Confederacy, also known as the Haudenosaunee, thrashed out their differences this way: every decision taken by the five tribes in council had to be unanimous. The Zapatistas in Mexico meet and debate decisions in the consulta until something as close as possible to unanimity is achieved.

And, impressively, consensus was the technique used during the planning of the Camp for Climate Action at Heathrow in 2007. According to one of the planners, they split up into five main working groups, which focused on: outreach, media and networking; the workshop programme; site practicalities; process/facilitation; and finance. The groups would all operate on a consensus basis and if there were disagreements – as, for example, with the press strategy, where some members wanted to keep journalists out altogether while others wanted to grant limited access – they just carried on talking until they could reach an agreement. They would then meet as a central group and bring each other up to date with developments. "It takes a long time," she says, and looks slightly exhausted by the memory (one meeting went on for a whole weekend), "but once you've agreed, everyone owns the decision. It's pretty inspiring." And Matthew Herbert of Seeds for Change agrees. "In the end you save time, because no one goes away irritated or hard done by, muttering and lobbying other members to go back and reverse the decision." It's not for everyone, but it's an interesting model.

On the day of the meeting, make sure you get to the venue early in order to turn the heating on, set up chairs, put out agendas and generally flap and angst that no one's going to turn up. Why did you do this? You could have been at home watching the latest episode of Heroes … until people start arriving. You'll know some of them, of course, but as strangers arrive you should immediately introduce yourself and anyone in your vicinity: you need this group to work together in beautiful harmony. Get people sitting down, and try to start, as far as possible, on time. There's plenty of time to chat in the pub afterwards.

This is a suggestion – just a suggestion! I am not trying, in any crypto-fascist-bourgeois sort of way, to dictate how you run your meeting or how the agenda for your first meeting should look.

1. Welcome speech

The facilitator's introduction should go something like this: "Hello, everyone, very pleased to see you. My name is [whatever] and I'm going to be facilitating this meeting. In future we'd like to rotate the position, but for this very first meeting it seems easier to just get ourselves up and running. I'd really like to get through the whole agenda before we have to be out of here, so I'm going to be very tough about time, and there may be occasions when we have to cut off discussions or questions. Please don't think I'm being rude – if issues arise that need further discussion and we haven't got time for them, then perhaps we can discuss them afterwards, or put them on the agenda for the next meeting." Arrange for someone to take minutes, if you want a record. It can also be useful to have a time-keeper to make sure each part of the meeting runs to schedule. Seeds for Change also suggests having a "vibes-watcher" – someone who watches the meeting in order to pick up dissatisfaction, irritation etc, so that issues can be dealt with quickly before people give up and leave the organisation. But it does require a certain sensitivity, and means yet more manpower. It's optional.

2. Introductions

So long as the group is not too big (more than 20 people makes this a bit unworkable), it's a good idea to get everyone to introduce themselves and explain why they've come. It breaks the ice a bit too. I don't personally favour those theatre game things where you throw balls to each other, or fall off tables, but each to their own. As one of the most important parts of any good campaign is its address book (you'll need to get in touch with all these people over and over again), you should also pass around a clipboard or individual contact sheets. At an absolute minimum, ask everyone present to write down their full name, phone number and email address. Postal addresses are useful and you might ask what people are willing to do for the campaign, eg hand out leaflets, staff stalls, etc.

3. Agenda and rules

The facilitator now moves on to the agenda, makes sure everyone is happy with it, and sets the basic rules for the meeting – hands up for questions, no swearing, no interrupting or whatever you prefer – with everyone's agreement. At this point you need to decide if you are going to run the campaign by majority vote or on the consensus system. If there are large numbers, then majority voting probably appeals, but the consensus system is good for building group spirit: it basically means finding a solution that everyone agrees with. It can also be useful to introduce people to the signal for general agreement, which takes a little getting used to but is incredibly useful once you stop feeling silly: you just tip your hands up, palms forward, and wave them both while someone is talking. If you disagree, you dangle them downwards and wave, palms inwards. It looks very silly but in a reasonably sized group is a good way of quickly taking the temperature on an issue without going through yet more discussion.

4. The issue

It sometimes works well for someone to stand up and give a little presentation about the problem in hand. It should be very jargon-free and unpatronising, just to make sure everyone is up to speed with the area you're talking about and won't be inhibited from joining in later. Perhaps if a neighbouring town has already defeated a similar planning application, you could get someone from that group in to talk to you about it. If you're forming a climate change action group, maybe get someone who has expert knowledge – perhaps they've been on a trip to the Arctic, or they work in the Met Office, or they've set up their own group – to give a short talk. But beware – if they're bad speakers, or go on for hours, you'll turn everyone off, so make sure you vet them beforehand and make them promise to speak for no more than 10 minutes, and ideally five.

I don't know why, but having a speaker gives people a kind of rest between getting themselves to the meeting and actually speaking. It also helps focus their minds and makes it feel like a proper evening out, too.

Why I fight

Bernadette Vallely
Founder of the Women's Environmental Network

My mum used to say "Why can't you get a normal job in banking or something?" But when I founded the Women's Environmental Network in 1988 I knew I was doing the right thing. I was inspired by my goddesses – Gaia and Tara, the Tibetan Buddhist goddess. I could sense a connection between women and the environment and I wanted to investigate it.

It was all so taboo. I used to give talks to women all around the country, focusing on the chlorine content of their sanitary protection. I'd throw sanitary towels – new ones, of course – into the audience, and everyone would squeal and say, "Eurgh!" They'd all been using these things all their life but they'd never actually opened them up and seen the plastic inside. When I brought out a book, The Sanitary Protection Scandal, the following year, I did an interview for ITN where we were only allowed to refer to sanitary towels as "soft tissue". Within a few days the main manufacturers had agreed to lower the chlorine levels.

I was also pilloried as an idiot for trying to persuade women to use cotton nappies for their babies. There isn't enough pulp in the

---

world for everyone on this planet to use disposable nappies, but women were telling me, "It's my right to use them." They didn't seem to understand how privileged they were. Reusable nappies were dying out then. I talked to the only company manufacturing them at that point and they just laughed at me, but now I see so many different types of reusable nappies available, it's wonderful.

I can feel the Goddess in every single drop of earth and every huge tree. Life is all about a balance between the masculine and the feminine, but for the last couple of thousand years the masculine has dominated – and that is an environmental disaster.

5. Aims

Now you want to establish your aims. Obviously if you've met because you want to stop a supermarket expansion, then this section of the meeting can be quite short: you just want to stop it. But for anything more complicated, it's worth breaking up into smaller discussion groups, handing out paper and pens and getting each group to come up with their top five priorities. Set a strict time limit, and ask each group to choose someone to take notes. They will then report back to the meeting at large. When that happens, collect all the aims on your board. So, a group that is trying to improve their neighbourhood may have: set up regular group, try to get a playground, get everyone recycling more, have a local newsletter, get rid of the dog poo, chase off the fly-posters, tidy up the park, cut down traffic, no more drug users, more police, improve bus service, need decent cycle lanes, get the borough's carbon footprint down ... Aaargh! You can end up with 50 different aims. How are you going to narrow them down?

Obviously it will vary in each situation. Can the different aims be themed – into, for example, the park, environmental concerns, crime issues, general litter, traffic issues, and administration of the campaign group itself (telephone numbers, arranging meetings, collecting the biscuit money, etc). Then, can these themes be handled by different working groups? If there aren't enough of you to do that, and you have very limited resources, then perhaps you can vote, or decide by consensus, on your favourite issues. Try to end up with a manageable list. It's a good feeling if you can get this bit finished off, rather than referring it to another meeting: it creates clarity and will help to keep things moving.

6. Targets and allies

This is the part where you establish who to contact, in order to get your aims met. If you are setting up a campaign against the building of a coal-fired power station nearby, then you need to establish who your campaign is aimed at. The company building the power station? The government? Or the local authority? If you don't have any information about these bodies, then deputise someone to go away and do some research, to get names, addresses, etc. If you're considering some kind of direct action, then any information about meetings, conferences and so on would also be useful. I once went to an anti-aviation direct action meeting where they decided to target the then transport secretary, Douglas Alexander, rather than the aviation industry. They discovered Alexander was going to address a conference of aviation bods the following month, which let them kill two birds with one stone.

If you're planning to improve your neighbourhood, at this point you'll be wanting to identify who your allies might be in the council and the local police service. Perhaps you'll also want to make contact with head teachers, or local businesses and newspapers. Again, some research may be necessary.

7. Break

You'll need some relief after all that brainstorming, and a meeting isn't a meeting without some kind of snackery. If there's no tea urn, then bring a kettle yourself, and try to organise some biscuits as a bare minimum. Take 15-30 minutes to scoff as much as you can, and make sure everyone's at least had a cuppa before the serious work resumes. Did you remember to bring soya milk/cow's milk and herbal tea/PG Tips? If not, there may be the odd wry shake of the head. Chuh!

8. Tactics

This is where you decide what you are actually going to do. Once again, you may want to split into smaller groups to make discussions easier, and then come back to the main meeting after 15 minutes or so to go through your ideas.

Mark Farmaner of the Burma Campaign warns that a lot of campaigns waste their energies setting up websites and newsletters and writing letters to newspapers. Unless you have identified these as priority aims – for example, you want to inform the public about that uranium mine or improve neighbourhood cohesion – then you need to be focused about what you're doing. The fewer things you try to do, the better you will do them.

Are you contemplating direct action? Then you need to come up with some imaginative ideas about what that action might be. Do you want to lobby your local council? Do you want to organise a neighbourhood party?

Bring everyone back together and go through the ideas. If you can't decide on a final course of action at this point, that's fine – especially as the research that you'll be doing now may bring up new possibilities. Just try to narrow it down a bit.

9. Who does what?

Set the assignments: get people to volunteer for the research and information-gathering, or whatever tasks you have all decided need doing. Bear in mind that if this is a long-term campaign, you want to try to increase the skill level too. If you've got one person who always writes the press releases, it's worth getting someone less experienced to help them: that way they'll pick up how to do it and when your expert goes awol you'll have back-up.

10. The next meeting

Agree on your next meeting now, while you're all together. It's infinitely quicker than trying to do it over the phone.

11. Any other business?

Allow a few minutes for any final thoughts, and then you should all head off for a drink. The pub is often the place where most gets done.

By the way, did you notice? You appear to have a plan.

The law and ... databases

The Data Protection Act of 1998 has a reputation for causing all sorts of absurd problems. Don't worry too much about the subtleties, however: just remember its existence when you are building up databases about the members of your campaign. Personal information (particularly "sensitive" data, which means a person's political persuasion, sexual orientation, religious beliefs, trade union status, physical or mental health, racial or ethnic origin, and criminal history) is, as it says, protected. Remember the eight principles of data handling: it must be fairly and lawfully processed; processed for limited purposes; adequate, relevant and not excessive; accurate and up to date; not kept for longer than is necessary; processed in line with your rights; secure; not transferred to other countries without adequate protection. Personal data must be kept secure, although there are some organisations – the police, for example – who may be permitted to ask you for the data if they think it will help them prevent a crime. The subject has the right to ask for the information which you hold about them. And it's an offence to pass it on to a third party (even a like-minded campaigning group) without the subject's permission. The easiest time to ask for this, of course, is when you're collecting the data.

Chapter Three
Fundraising

At some point in your campaign you are going to need resources, space and money: how much depends very much on what you want to do. You may want 40 quid to make some flyers, a couple of hundred pounds so you can create a newsletter, or thousands in order to pursue legal action. For detailed guidance on fundraising, you'd do well to get in touch with the Directory of Social Change (DSC), the Institute of Fundraising (IoF) and the National Council for Voluntary Organisations (NCVO), all of which produce texts full of expert advice. The DSC is particularly useful when fundraising for small groups. There are plenty of fiddly regulations that need to be heeded, and you must be thorough about these things. If you're putting on a play, for example, and you fail the fire inspection, the whole thing will be shut down. But here are a few suggestions for getting started.

The **whip-round** is the most traditional technique – asking everyone to chuck a tenner into the pot. If you have a newsletter or a website you'll want to mention the constant need for cash there, and make sure you include information about how money can be given to the group. Perhaps you can set up a membership scheme and include an annual charge. You can extend this as far as you can stand it: taking a collecting tin down to the town centre on a Saturday perhaps (see The law and ... fundraising, at the end of this chapter) or doing a few pub collections (always ask the pub staff for permission first). Don't hassle people! Causing annoyance is illegal. Always, always smile.

Fundraising events are also a great way to get people involved and to raise your campaign's profile. But Carole Barbone, champion fundraiser behind the group Stop Stansted Expansion, points out that your reputation is all-important: people are more likely to give you money if they trust you to spend it wisely.

It's essential to be creative and properly entertaining. The Stansted bunch come up with new wheezes all the time, from "runway rambles" (walks in the Essex countryside around Stansted airport) to teddy bears' picnics and family cycle rides. You could throw a gig with local bands or have a garden party: take stock of your assets and then think as big as possible. Don't forget to have collectors wandering around: squeeze every penny out of the public that you possibly can. Sponsored events can be surprisingly lucrative. Perhaps you can get everyone on a sponsored walk, run, climb or even silence. If you get 30 people involved and they all raise £100, that's £3,000 right there.

Some other ideas could include an art show, a sponsored non-uniform day (with all the children at a school paying 50p to wear their normal clothes), a play, an open house day, an auction, window-cleaning, karaoke night, a ping-pong/tennis/darts tournament, a barn dance, a jumble sale, a cabaret night, cake stalls, a read-a-thon, a car wash day, a big dinner or even a banquet, or perhaps a dinner dance, a barbecue, a treasure hunt, a fashion show, a raffle, a sports day, a fantastic fireworks party … Make sure you sell tickets in advance, so you don't end up sitting in an empty hall on the day feeling crushed. Lots of local advertising, energy and planning are needed.

You'll be amazed at how easily you can **get stuff for free**, too, particularly if you're running a campaign to improve your local area. You could come up with a wish list, for example, and put it on your website. Or you could plead with local businesses and offer them advertising if you're going to set up a website or free sheet. They can give you prizes if you're doing a raffle, or provide food if you're putting on a party. Look out for opportunities – one campaign was offered the use of a marquee for free the day after a wedding, so it held a fine wine appreciation event and raised hundreds.

Another wheeze is **trading**: if you have a design genius in your ranks this could be a doozy. The 2007 Camp for Climate Action could have cleaned up with T-shirts emblazoned This Planet Has No Emergency Exit, although this might have clashed with its anti-consumer principles. Stop Stansted Expansion has made thousands from a calendar of beauty spots that would be wiped out if the airport was enlarged. Posters, postcards, bags (one manufacturer told me that if you come up with a campaign logo and put in a minimum order of 250, it will print up sturdy cotton shoppers at £1.02 a bag – so if you sell them for £3 you'll nearly triple your money), lunchboxes, wallets … Imagination is required once more, and quite a lot of graft where the selling is concerned. If you're having a fundraising event, or even a meeting, make sure you've got plenty of stock.

Why I fight

Rebecca Lush Blum
Anti-road protestor

I was supposed to be studying politics at Bristol, but a few people had just set up camp in protest against the M3 across Twyford Down, which is where I grew up. It was really the first road protest, back in 1992, and everyone there was unbelievably idealistic: the feeling was, "Well, this might not work but I'm going to have a go anyway." I started going every weekend. I was going to these dry, dusty lectures about politics at university, and then I was seeing real politics in action at the camp. Eventually I dropped out and just moved to the camp full-time.

The campaign got more and more high-profile and when I ended up serving two weeks in Holloway prison for breaking an injunction not to be at the site, the European commissioner for the environment actually came to visit me. I was getting 100 letters a day. It was obvious that there was a lot of support out there for what we were doing.

The protests went on for the next five years, and although the media focused mainly on the defeats, we really forced the Tories to back down. When we'd started the actions, there had been 600 roads in the pipeline, but by the time we finished they'd been whittled away down to 150, and when New Labour came in they promised to suspend the entire road-building programme. By any standards, that is a successful campaign.

Since then, of course, Labour has been slowly bringing the roads back, and now there are over 200 schemes planned. In 2005 they announced that they were going to build a motorway between Birmingham and Manchester – trashing the Staffordshire countryside, basically. Even the Tories never did anything that bad. I just thought, "That's enough."

So I got in touch with the people I knew from the first time around and asked for help to start Roadblock, and everyone was extraordinarily generous. Everyone is really in despair about what's happened, that all that hard work has been unravelled. In 2007 Roadblock joined up with the Campaign for Better Transport, and now I concentrate on putting local groups in touch with each other, keeping up with policy announcements, and generally trying to get us organised at a national level. Small campaign groups working separately are too easy to pick off one by one.

However, you can get stung here: if you don't sell all the bags, for example, your time and effort will have been wasted. So it's best to do the trading thing if you can also make it perform another service. For example, if you're producing the bags as part of a project to get plastic bags out of your village, then they become more significant. If you're trying to help an impoverished Kurdish community in Turkey and you discover that they make lovely rugs, then selling those rugs on their behalf makes far more sense than just flogging some bags you had made up in Britain.

Doing these things on a small scale may work, but if you want to raise a lot of money you're going to have to become, in effect, a business, and you had better be ready to compete in the marketplace like everyone else. No one buys a rug because the people who made it are poor. That is the brutal truth.

Seeds for Change sensibly points out that "**going to work** is often easier, quicker and more lucrative than any of the above, but more often forgotten. Rather than spending 20 hours working on a mad scheme to get money, it's sometimes better to just go and work in a pub collecting glasses for 20 hours." This is how Camp Bling, the road protest camp in Essex, operates: almost all the protestors have full-time jobs.

The Women's Institute is one of the organisations that have made this approach a central plank of their fundraising. At the 2007 Tolpuddle Festival, for example, celebrating trade unionism in Dorset, the WI provided a lot of food, and did it absolutely fantastically: lunch in the village hall featured an absurdly wide range of quiches and salads and sandwiches, and one whole table devoted to cakes, all highly individual. The Workers Beer Company (WBC), meanwhile, manned the bars; this is one of the fundraising arms of the labour and trade union movement, designed to help grassroots organisations raise money. Founded in the 1980s with the slogan Thirst Among Equals, the WBC does the bars at festivals such as Glastonbury, Leeds and Reading. It'll take you on if it likes the sound of your campaign, and for every hour you work will pay £6.50 into your campaign bank account. If there are, say, four of you, and you each put in 20 hours over a festival, that's £520. Plus a free weekend at a festival ... There are worse ways to fill your coffers.

If things are starting to get serious, it might be worth looking around for a **grant**. The DSC produces the Directory of Grant-Making Trusts (price £99), and can give you tons of guidance about who to start talking to. It also has several databases to which you can subscribe, although the most important of them – the one that lists all the UK grant-making trusts – does cost more than £200 a year. The National Council for Voluntary Organisations (NCVO) tends to deal more with the large organisations looking to raise tens or hundreds of thousands. Grants Online also carries useful information about grant-making trusts around the country; again you need to subscribe to use its databases, which are usefully mapped out into specialist interests, from energy and environment, through rural development, to young people and families. The Government Funding website gives extremely useful information about getting grants from government departments. Other possible sources of information are companies like Guidestar and Funderfinder.

The national lottery gives out money to a wide variety of projects. And it might be worth applying to your local council as they will usually give grants to community and voluntary organisations. In Aberdeenshire, for example, the council distributes grants on behalf of the Carnegie Trust to village bodies doing local initiatives and rural projects. It also gives out grants of up to £15,000 to voluntary and community programmes.

Grant applications are time-consuming and difficult, however: if you dislike filling out forms you are really going to hate this. They can run to dozens of pages, and you need to be eloquent about the reasoning behind your campaign, focused on what you actually need the money for, and neat. Scribbling a few words in purple felt-tip tends to create a bad impression.

The law and ... fundraising

Obviously, there are rules for collecting money from people. There are laws that you must obey, and then there are codes of practice covering, for example, house-to-house collecting drawn up by the Institute of Fundraising. Although large chunks of the codes of practice are not compulsory, and/or apply to charities rather than small voluntary groups, it's worth complying with them wherever practical. They are based on years of experience. (And if you use paid fundraisers, even stricter rules apply.)

If you're planning a street collection, first contact your local authority (or, if you're in the Metropolitan police area, your local police station). Collections usually need to be licensed (the policy varies from authority to authority), as do some public events. Your local authority will also be able to tell you if you need a licence for a lottery or a raffle, whether as part of an event or as a fundraiser in its own right. Who you sell tickets to, and when and where, will all make a difference. Large lotteries must be licensed by the Gambling Commission, which has a helpline.

Perhaps you've jumped through all these hoops and are itching to rattle the collecting tins? Not so fast. You must establish absolutely transparent procedures for dealing with the money: this is vital anyway, if you want to be trusted as an organisation. Donations are protected under law. It's no good just shoving them in a shoe box and hoping for the best.

When you are collecting, you need to explain extremely clearly what that money will be used for – so if you are doing a sponsored run and some of the donations will pay for organising the run, this should be clearly stated. Money must be used in the way the donor was told – if not, it must be returned or permission sought (and a record kept of this) to use it in another way.

When you've done a collection and emptied out the money on to a table back at HQ, the IoF suggests that two unrelated people (eg, not a brother and sister, or a married couple) should always count it together, and that they should bring the accounts up to date on the same occasion, rather than leaving it till later. Legally, you are not allowed to make any deductions from the donations: if you're owed expenses, you need to get them back from the organisation later, rather than just taking the money out of the pot.

It's also best to set up a bank account with two or more designated signatories. The bank may require you to have a constitution, which should state why the fund was set up and what will happen to the money if the group disbands, etc.

There's no legal obligation to keep accounts, but it is important to take bookkeeping seriously if you plan to apply for grants or funds at some point, or to register as a charity. In any case, keeping the money straightforward saves arguments and mistrust, both of which are absolutely fatal to morale.

What about becoming a charity, though? This is only possible if your organisation's income is over £5,000 a year, so it probably won't be one of your first concerns. On the plus side, charitable status means tax breaks and usually makes fundraising easier. On the minus, charities are governed by all sorts of laws that don't apply to voluntary groups, including the need to file annual returns and have their accounts audited. Other methods of getting external endorsement include becoming a member of the Institute of Fundraising (a very helpful lot), or getting the FRSB tick from the Fundraising Standards Board. It costs about £30 to join if you're a small organisation.

... and public events

Finally, a few things to bear in mind for fundraising parties, gigs and so on:

Fire hazards: You need to have an evacuation plan for the venue, and be aware of the location of the fire exits. Contact your local fire service for help.

Access: The law allows for the fact that it may be impractical to create access for wheelchair users, for example, but you need to try.

First aid: Make sure there is a basic medical kit on the premises, as well as someone trained in first aid. You may want to contact St John's Ambulance, who provide first aid cover for big events: they can advise you on the extent of cover you need.

Food preparation: Under food safety laws, if you're planning to sell food at your party you need to follow hygiene procedures. Wash your hands frequently, keep your hair covered, keep the surfaces clean. Don't let raw meat touch other food – use different chopping boards. You need to display notices of what is in the food as well, in order to avoid allergic reactions.

Serving booze: You need a licence, unless your venue already has one. You may need one for food and music, too. Speak to your local authority.

Chapter Four
Petitions

In the dog days of 2003, Cadbury discontinued a bubbly chocolate bar called the Wispa. The earth did not move. Most of Britain seemed resigned to this cruel twist of fate, including the blogger Dave Simpson, who wrote a moving farewell to the "velvety textured milk chocolate". "I went in search of the last remaining Wispas which are working their way through the newsagent shelves," he wrote. "I was prepared for a long search through the back streets of London, but found my favourite local newsagents on Charlotte Street had a few in stock."

Although Cadbury said its Dairy Milk Bubbly was almost identical, Simpson lamented that it "hasn't the same crunch as the old Wispa. This is mostly due to its lack of girth. I remember queueing up to get my Wispas as a teenager from my old school tuck shop, which intriguingly operated out of the science block windows. And so another part of history dies ... "

But Simpson was wrong. Over the following months the word went out far and wide, and petitions were set up around the country to bring back the Wispa. At the Gopetition campaigners' website at least four petitions were launched – although a single one might have made more sense – while other Wispa-lovers later set up Facebook groups and posted messages on YouTube. Over four years the campaign, amazingly, grew and grew, with feelings running so high that in 2007 two fans stormed the stage during Iggy Pop's Glastonbury gig waving a Bring Back Wispa banner.

Finally Cadbury gave in, and announced in September 2007 that it would bring the Wispa back in order to see if demand held up. A spokesman said at the time: "We get letters about the Aztec bar and the lime barrel in the Dairy Milk tray [which fell victim to previous rationalisations]. But this is on a whole different scale. This is the first time we are going to give the internet a chance to prove itself and see whether it is all hype or genuine." The company made 23m Wispas and put them on the shop shelves in October. Petitions: they really do work.

And they've never been easier to set up, thanks to email and the internet. Social networking sites such as Facebook and MySpace are a-swill with campaigns and petitions, ranging from the frivolous to the deeply serious. Some have tens of thousands of supporters (although I notice with great sadness that Stop Garden Gnome Oppression has only 475. Where is the love?). Over at Care2, an enormous activists' network with more than seven million members, a petition for a Universal Declaration on Animal Welfare has 58,000 signatures. And AVAAZ (which means "voice" in many asian, middle eastern and eastern European languages) is a global "web movement" which claims to have 3.5 million members. They deliver some simply colossal petitions, by just emailing those 3.5 million people and asking them to sign – they got 800,000 signatures on a petition urging the UN Security Council to oppose the violent response of the Burmese authorities to the protests of the monks in October 2007.

Some people are rather sniffy about petitions: the doughty political campaigner Ron Bailey, for example, dismisses parliamentary petitions as being pretty much pointless, while a Hansard Society survey of MPs in 2003 found that only 3 per cent thought of them as a "highly effective" way of putting issues before the House of Commons. But that seems odd to me. Petitions are a powerful means of doing three things: building up a database of supporters, weighing up public interest in an issue, and making the levels of public support clear to the government (or the corporation, or whoever you are petitioning).

Perhaps the problem is that they seem old-fashioned: they are, in many ways, the original campaigning tool. To begin with, petitioning just meant to put your problem before the emperor or king: the word derives from the Latin *petere* – to aim at, lay claim to. They were the only way most people had of raising their problems with a higher authority. In the Middle Ages in England, the king would get petitions about money he owed someone, or an army that had taken up residence in a prelate's church, or soldiers' wages that were not being paid. They ranged from the straightforward, such as a request from Edward I's cook, John de Wautham, "who has long served first the king's father, and then his brothers, Thomas and Edmund" to be supported in his old age by the priory of Hatfield Broad Oak, to the extraordinary, such as a plea from Idonea le Furmager, daughter of Godfrey le Furmager (the cheesemonger) for Edward II to punish the man who had raped her as a child. The relationship of subject and monarch was never questioned, the ruler's right to hand down any verdict never doubted. More than four centuries and a civil war later, the right to petition the monarch was still considered important enough to be enshrined in the 1689 English Bill of Rights.

Why I fight

Nick Mercer
Tours festivals with demonstrations of renewable energy and recycling

The Campaign for Real Events voluntary organisation actually started life as a front for putting on punk gigs back in the 1980s and has been through many different incarnations since. At heart it's always been driven by my interest in refuse and waste as both material and inspiration for constructive projects. I'm fascinated with renewable energy and disgusted that so much stuff is being thrown away, so many of the things I've built have been energy generators.

I started with pedal-powered sound systems which were used at festivals and street events. Whenever we announced that the batteries were running low you'd always get a crowd of kids running forwards. The adult sized bikes were too big for them so I built some child-sized ones but found that it was quite hard to inter-face them with the sound system. So I started attaching them to things that children might be interested in.

My favourite machine is the Inflatable Bin-Liner Monster. One day I was at a camp in Pontefract, a precursor to the Northern Green Gathering. Between meetings we connected a pedal gener-ator to an old computer fan in a broken bucket and built a basic figure with arms and a smiley face from bin liners and insulating tape. Another popular application with the kids is a directly powered Nintendo game. At first they don't believe it's possible, then forget to pedal every time they get to a difficult bit in the game and even-tually enjoy the challenge. Recently we've been booked as children's entertainment at many events as well as energy education projects in schools.

Other renewable energy projects have included a solar powered backpack PA system which allows electric instruments to be played in processions, and night time processions in which lanterns and recycled Christmas lights are powered from solar charged batteries. In between the fifteen or so events and workshops we do each year, I also fit in a full time job as a hospital technician. Someone once asked me why I do it. I suppose that if I can see something's worth doing, I just get quite determined about it.

What if you want to set up a petition today? First, **decide who it is for.** If it's a corporation you want to tackle, then you just set it up and send it in. The company is under no legal obligation to respond to you, but if it has any sense (ie, if you have gathered enough signatures to make it worry about its sales) it will. Public opinion may not have counted for much in the Middle Ages, but it certainly does now. Just look at Cadbury's response to the Wispa campaign.

Political petitions now are usually addressed to parliament, rather than the monarch. If you want to petition the House of Commons yourself, a comprehensive list of rules is available from the clerk for public petitions in the House of Commons, and you're advised to run your petition past that office before you send it in, to make sure you've got it right. In short:

1. Your petition must be respectfully addressed to the House of Commons.
2. Each signatory must include his/her address.
3. Each petition must contain a "prayer" – a request that the House of Commons is capable of granting.
4. There must be a suitable closing phrase.

Your petition must be put before the Commons during a special slot at the end of the day. You need to approach your local MP to help you with this: he or she is duty-bound to present it, but if they're not particularly interested, they can just lob it into a special bag that hangs off the back of the Speaker's chair. If, however, they think it's worth a mention, they'll present it to the house in person.

There's a long tradition of bringing petitions to the prime minister's front door if you wish to petition him or her directly. Again, the petition should include your request: the usual format is "We, the undersigned, petition the prime minister to ... perform Careless Whisper at our karaoke night". Or whatever. Nowadays you can also go via cyberspace, in the form of the **Downing Street e-petition site**. Just how effective this can be was shown by the 2007 anti-road-pricing campaign. No sooner had the government begun the consultation process on this extremely sensitive subject than the motoring lobby scared up 1.7m signatures against any kind of road pricing at any point ever. Cue much chicken-with-head-cut-offness by politicians, to the point where Tony Blair himself wrote one of his heartfelt personal messages in answer to the petition: "Before we take any decisions about a national pricing scheme, we know that we have to have a system that works. A system that respects our privacy as individuals. A system that is fair. I fully accept that we don't have all the answers yet ... " The whole thing was seen as a public relations disaster for Downing Street, and much unseemly rejoicing took place.

But actually, after this initial hitch, the Downing Street e-petition website has now become a wonderful, if unscientific, way of taking the political temperature: it's an enjoyable way of giving yourself a reality check about people's preoccupations, and is getting thousands of petitions a month (unlike the parliamentary system, which gets a couple of hundred a year, max). Sadly, joke petitions are no longer accepted, but in one day, for example, petitions demanding that wolves be reintroduced to the Scottish Highlands will be posted alongside calls to ban WiFi in schools, to require television broadcasters to remove on-screen logos, and to create a "none of the above" option on ballot papers – at least two of which I'd consider signing up for. One petition asked that Jeremy Clarkson become prime minister "because Jezza is legend and deserves a chance to run the country". Downing Street, in a rare and wonderful burst of good humour responded with a YouTube video which said politely over a shot of number 10 Downing Street: "Thanks to the 49,447 people who signed the petition to "Make Jeremy Clarkson prime minister". You made a compelling case, and we thought long and hard about it," – at this point the video camera panned up the stairs inside number 10, past pictures of previous prime ministers including Margaret Thatcher and John Major to reveal Clarkson's photograph, at which point the video states firmly – "But on second thoughts ... maybe not."

Perhaps because of jealousy that the prime minister's getting all the good petitions now, the House of Commons procedures committee has been taking another look at the way petitions are submitted to parliament, and has suggested that the government make a commitment to respond to all of them within two months. The hope is clearly that this might help with Gordon Brown's plans to "reinvigorate democracy", and the communities minister Hazel Blears is also looking into ways of building petitions into local government, by obliging local authorities to respond to those with a certain number of signatures.

And that road-pricing scheme? The one against which the British people rose in petitionary form? Shelved. A statement was released by the Department for Transport, very quietly in October 2007, stating: "It is not the department's intention, at this stage, to take the separate powers needed to price the national road network." It was raised again by the Committee on Climate Change in early 2009, but any government who suggests adopting this as policy knows that there is already a network of people out there ready to spring into action against it.

Yup. As I said earlier, petitions really can work.

Ctrl.Alt.Shift: September 11 2009

Today the government said sorry for something it had done wrong because we asked them to.

It all goes back a long way to the second world war, where a mathematician called Alan Turing was one of our "code-crackers", one of the brainiacs who managed to break the Enigma code that the Germans were using to send each other messages. The cracking of this code was one of the absolutely pivotal moments of the war, and enabled the allies to set up their final invasion while closely monitoring German movements. In other words, without Turing's work the war might have turned out very, very differently.

But Turing was gay, and in those days homosexuality was regarded as criminal, even as a form of madness. Just a few years later in 1952 Turing was convicted of "gross indecency" and then chemically castrated. This was an experimental treatment on "sex offenders" which involved giving them medication in order to reduce their sex drive. Two years later Turing (clearly driven to despair by having his very core questioned and criminalised), committed suicide.

A little while ago, however, a man called John Graham-Cumming decided to put a petition up on the e-petitions website in memory of Turing. He did this with a message saying: "If 500 people sign it, there will eventually be a response from the government to the petition." A few more than 500 people signed it, with the total as of 4pm on Friday 10 September standing at more than 31,000. And, duly prompted, the government has actually, amazingly listened. It is a simple matter; this was wrong. And so they have apologised.

One lesson from this and one thought.

The lesson: petitions really do work, if enough people sign them. Graham-Cumming did no publicity for his petition, but it was about a course of events so straightforwardly wrong that we all know, as a matter of simple human justice, that we must sign.

The thought: it makes no difference to Alan Turing whatsoever. But it will make a difference to the thousands of gay or lesbian men and women around the world who are persecuted for their very identities. Do not underestimate the importance of solidarity.

Chapter Five
Demonstrations

To organise a demonstration is the simplest thing in the world. You decide where you're going to meet. You decide if you're going to walk somewhere else (this turns it into a march as well). You get in touch with as many people as possible to get them to come along. You show up. This is a demonstration.

If you want, of course, there can be more to it that that. You can add a few "happenings" – bands, speakers, fire-breathers (the jugglers usually turn up without being asked). You can spend lots of time getting people there, so it's larger and more impressive. You can do a huge publicity campaign, you can come up with slogans and brands and databases. Even all this can still be done in a fairly short timespan.

In the States in 2007, Bill McKibben and the Step It Up organisation put together 1,400 demos against climate change around the country in about 10 weeks. Along the south end of the island of Manhattan, hundreds of protestors dressed in wetsuits formed a human shoreline, sometimes running several blocks inland, to show the expensive real estate that would be reclaimed as sea levels rose. In Jacksonville, Florida, one group hoisted a yacht from a crane to show where the water would come up to if nothing was done. Off the coast, divers demonstrated underwater to highlight the threat to the reefs. It was a wonderful bit of popular mobilisation.

But a very **basic demo** can be legally organised, from start to finish, in a couple of days. All you need is enough time to make a couple of calls, drop a letter of notification round to the police station in whose jurisdiction you will be marching (it should, ideally, be delivered a week in advance but if you drop it off by hand then a couple of days is acceptable) and, obviously, paint the banner. (Banner-painting is one of the unavoidable bits of protesting. Lots of people hate it, but every so often you get one person who really enjoys mucking around with bits of fabric and sloppy poster paints: they are a treasure and must be cherished.) I think we are under the illusion that demos can only be organised by professionals, but actually they are open to anyone, no qualification needed.

Because it's what comes naturally when you have a grievance – to gather in a crowd and let the authorities know – people have demonstrated and rioted for as long as we've existed: there were dozens of slave revolts in ancient Greece and Rome, and medieval peasants were always given to a good punch up if they were unhappy about something. But historian EP Thompson believes that in the UK, after the events of 1688 where the rioting London mob unnerved the idiotic King James II into an early retreat and allowed the Dutch William I to step in smoothly and take over, men and women felt "that the Glorious Revolution afforded a constitutional precedent for the right to riot in resistance to oppression".

Throughout the 18th century the British crowd was famous for its turbulence, for its food riots and industrial disputes, and, despite the most punitive criminal code in Europe, for what historian Ian Gilmour has called its "sturdy disrespect for its superiors". When George I took the throne in 1715, he was told by his private secretary Robethon that if the "very changeable ... populace" were on the side of the court it had nothing to fear, whereas if they were against, the court was "never safe". The crowds could unite on conservative issues, or in order to press for reform of unjust laws, but their influence was felt at all levels, as prime minister Robert Walpole discovered in 1733 when an outbreak of window-breaking and rioting forced him to abandon plans to increase the tax on tobacco and salt. As the century wore on, tectonic plates were shifting beneath the surface; the old hierarchical land-owning world with its patriarchal protections for the poor was slowly being dismantled and replaced by a market world where the industrialists and capitalists would have control. In the 1790s there was fiery confrontation between a population with increasingly radical demands for parliamentary reform and even universal suffrage, and a nervous government (watching the French Revolution just across the Channel): the resulting Combination Acts, which made it illegal to gather for the purpose of raising wages or improving working conditions, were a direct challenge to the public's right to demonstrate.

Why I fight

Jill Grieve

Helped to organise the September 2002 Countryside March, which brought about 400,000 protestors to London

I joined the Countryside Alliance in 1999. It had been founded in 1997 when people realised that Labour just didn't have a clue about the countryside, so we had better let them know. We had already had a march in 1998, and there was supposed to be another one in 2001 but because of foot and mouth we had to cancel that. So in 2002 people really wanted to make themselves heard. There were hunting bills flying around all over the place, and everybody felt very let down, as if we weren't being listened to.

The day of the march was just wonderful. I remember standing on the corner of Trafalgar Square with the hairs on the back of my neck standing up and this wall of people moving along in front of me. They came from everywhere: people came down from the north of Scotland, and they caught ferries from Newcastle, and they got up at three in the morning to drive up from Cornwall. The whole world seemed to be watching, too: I remember talking to a journalist who'd come all the way from Argentina to cover it.

I think people were fascinated because hunting is something that's so strongly tied up with the English identity: one man told me that when he thinks of England he thinks of hunting. My favourite moment was probably seeing my family coming towards me; they'd brought a picnic and they had bottles of wine in their pockets. And I loved seeing all the kids everywhere. The stereotype was that it was all going to be red-faced toffs, and actually there were children everywhere you looked – it was all about family and really inclusive, and I loved that. There was even a couple in their wedding clothes – they'd got married the day before and come down to join the march that day. It was a really warm atmosphere – it was amazing to feel that everybody there was with you, and that you weren't alone.

Even though we lost the battle over the hunting bill, the march gave us a powerful voice, and there are a lot of areas now where we can make a difference. Post offices, farming, fly-tipping, local food – these are all areas that are of vital importance to rural people.

That right was only finally encoded in British law in 1998 with the Human Rights Act. But it has always been considered fundamental to our society; it could be thought of as one of the assumed terms of the British social contract.

Nowadays it is an international right, too. Article 21 of the International Covenant on Civil and Political Rights, published by the United Nations in 1966, declares: "The right of peaceful assembly shall be recognised. No restrictions may be placed on the exercise of this right other than those imposed in conformity with the law and which are necessary in a democratic society in the interests of national security or public safety, public order (*ordre public*), the protection of public health or morals or the protection of the rights and freedoms of others." When that right is threatened or denied, and soldiers fire on unarmed protestors – as in Tiananmen Square, or more recently in Burma – it is seen as one of the greatest crimes a state can commit.

A march is still one of the most powerful ways that a movement has of making itself felt. The Make Poverty History campaign, for example, was centred on the meeting of the G8 at Gleneagles in Scotland in July 2005. The cause – social and economic justice for developing nations – had been building momentum and credibility, and politicians were increasingly desperate to come on board and be associated with the message (Hilary Benn, then secretary of state for international development, actually joined the march). In Edinburgh on July 2 2005 some 225,000 people – the equivalent of half the city's population – marched through the streets calling for the G8 to deliver trade justice and drop the debt. The sheer size of the march dispelled any remaining suspicions that the issue could be brushed away, and within a couple of days the politicians had announced an aid package. That, you see, is what marches do: a good turnout demonstrates beyond all doubt that a cause has serious support – look, here are the bodies to prove it. (You can argue for ever about whether the aid package that the G8 delivered was actually of any worth, or whether Make Poverty History sold its more radical goals down the river. But, as one of the marchers put it: "I'd rather be arguing about whether what they did was any use, than feeling depressed because they hadn't done anything at all.")

Yet there's no denying that the reputation of demos and marches has taken a huge knock in the past few years. I started discussing politics recently with a London cabby (I know, I know – next time I'll remember to start chewing my own hand off first). Having had a good rant about the political apathy in our nation – "You look at those people at that bus stop over there: if you ask them what they think about politics they'll just say, 'I dunno'" – he then said that no, he'd never really been bothered enough about anything to go on a march himself. "It doesn't really make any difference, does it? I mean, you look at that anti-Iraq war march. That didn't stop the war, did it?

What's the point of us having less cars when the developing world has got coal fumes coming out their ears?"

The anti-war demonstrations in February 2003 created a big headache for those who believe in taking action. Sometimes, they reminded us, no matter how many people take to the streets with you, the powers-that-be will not listen. On February 15 somewhere between eight and 30 million people poured into cities from Calcutta to Washington, bearing banners saying anything from "Impeach Bush" to "My Mum Reads the Daily Mail and Even She Says: Don't Attack Iraq". In Florida naked protestors gathered on the beaches. In Scotland 100,000 people marched through Glasgow. In London at least a million headed for a rally at Hyde Park. In Ireland another 100,000 marched through Dublin. In South Africa, President Thabo Mbeki led the protestors. It seemed like a huge unstoppable tidal wave of political pressure beneath which George W Bush and his allies must give way. And the result? Sod all. Worse than sod all. Condoleezza Rice, Bush's national security adviser, said the marches would not affect the administration's "determination to confront Saddam Hussein and help the Iraqi people" (and how very helpful the invasion has proved, after all!). The following day Tony Blair made a speech to the Labour party in Glasgow full of "moral" this and "moral" that, and including the immortal line "I do not seek unpopularity as a badge of honour". The speech was absolutely bankrupt, confounding al-Qaida with Saddam Hussein at every opportunity, trying to argue that Saddam's brutality justified invasion even without a UN mandate, and neatly sidestepping the widespread anxiety about the motivations behind the plan to invade Iraq. A month later, in a state of national depression, we watched the bombs fall.

Now, if all that got us nowhere, as my taxi driver pointed out, what exactly is the point? A whole group of people who had never protested before will probably never bother again. That is the problem with a mass mobilisation of that size: if it collapses and fails, it can take the wind out of the movement for a good long while.

But there are also arguments on the positive side. One peace protestor pointed out to me that the march did lead to "Wobbly Wednesday", the day when Rumsfeld suggested that perhaps the British wouldn't need to be involved, and there were many civil servants running about behind the scenes in Whitehall having last-minute nervous breakdowns. It is argued that perhaps it has slowed down the rate at which we rush into war with Iran. It has also been said that we're getting quicker at mobilising against war. The veteran activist and writer Noam Chomsky pointed out in late 2002 that "compared with the Vietnam war movement, this movement is just incomparably ahead now ... I can't think of an example in the entire history of Europe, including the United States, when there was ever protest of any substantial level before a war. Here you've got massive protest before war's even started. It's a tremendous tribute to changes in popular culture that have taken place in western countries in the last 30 or 40 years. It's just phenomenal." And Chomsky rarely does this much enthusiasm. So you have to put aside the failure of these particular anti-war demos. They are part of a whole movement, not an end in themselves, and as part of the peace movement they marked a step forward, not a step backwards.

Demonstrating is and always will be a fearsomely potent way of expressing the will of the people. At its most powerful it unsheathes a huge sword with the spine-tingling shing of metal that makes onlookers fall silent: you are reminded suddenly that if one side has broken its part of the social contract, then the other side can break it too. You are reminded where the muscle lies.

The law and ... demos and marches

Slightly different laws apply to demonstrations (static protests on public land) and processions/marches along a planned route.

For the former, the world's your oyster, as long as you're not planning on protesting within the "designated area" around parliament, in which case you'll need police permission. You must, however, make sure you are not obstructing the highway, which is any road or path over which the public has the right to pass and repass. This is a criminal offence under the Highways Act 1980. (This law does not apply to Northern Ireland but the police can arrest you for causing an "unlawful obstruction" on the road.) Make sure the demo remains polite and not threatening in any way, otherwise the demonstrators could be accused of aggravated trespass under the Criminal Justice and Public Order Act 1994. If you have more than six vehicles, under the same act, the police can ask you to leave. But remember: it is quite possible that if you are protesting peacefully and causing absolutely no disruption you will be left completely alone.

If you are organising a march, you need to begin by letting the police know. You need to give them the names and contact details of the organisers, as well as the date and time and the proposed route (bearing in mind that under the Serious Organised Police and Crime Act 2005 there are "designated areas" such as the area around Parliament where extra conditions exist) and you should, ideally, get this to them six clear days before the procession is to take place. If that's not possible, then do it by hand as soon as is reasonably practicable although be aware that legally, failure to deliver the details a week before could result in a prosecution. If it is a truly spontaneous march, then you may be exempt.

The police have the power to impose conditions on a march, or even to prohibit it completely, but it may be worth reminding them that you can dispute their decision through the courts. They must show that they believe the march may result in serious public disorder, serious damage to property or serious disruption to the life of the community, or that the organisers' purpose is "the intimidation of others with a view to compelling them not to do an act they have a right to do, or do an act they have a right not to do". If you fail to comply with police conditions, you could face up to three months in prison. And anyone who even goes on a march that has been banned – let alone continues to organise it – could also go down for three months. You don't mess with the boys in blue.

In Northern Ireland public protest meetings and processions are controlled by the Parades Commission. Under the Public Procession act 1998, you need to give 28 days notice of marches and 14 days notice of related political meetings: they can't ban you but they can reroute you. The Secretary of State for Northern Ireland may, however, ban marches if he deems it necessary.

... riot and disorder

Under the Public Order Act 1986, you're guilty of affray if you use or threaten to use unlawful violence against someone else – if 12 or more people do this, they can be charged with rioting or violent disorder, which carries up to 10 years imprisonment.

... banners and posters

Given the hassle involved in coming up with a slogan for your placards, then painting them and finding somewhere to keep them, it's worth remembering that they can, if misworded, get you in trouble. The Public Order Act 1986 prohibits the display of material that could be threatening, abusive or insulting to members of the public, or provoke violence, or cause members of the public to fear violence, or cause harassment, alarm or distress. In 2001 the peace protestor Lindis Percy and an evangelical Christian were both charged under this act, the former for defacing an American flag at a US airbase, the latter for displaying a placard reading "Stop Homosexuality, Stop Immorality, Stop Lesbianism". (Lindis Percy was cleared, the Christian, a 67 year old called Harry Hammond, was convicted.)

The Racial and Religious Hatred Act 2006 and the Criminal Justice and Immigration Act 2008 have further extended these offences to include stirring up hatred against persons on religious grounds and stirring up hatred on the grounds of sexual orientation. (This also applies to films, plays and written material.)

Common law and the Offence Against the Person Act 1861 also make it a crime to solicit murder, as one Londoner was reminded in 2006 when he was jailed for distributing placards bearing slogans such as "Annihilate those who insult Islam". It may be safer to stick with "Down With Brown".

... the police

The relationship between police and protestors is historically a bit sticky. The police should be more grateful, really: one of the reasons they were brought into being was the public uproar after the Peterloo Massacre in 1819, when local volunteer yeomanry were sent in to break up a political gathering. The yeomanry charged into the crowd with their sabres drawn, and 11 people were killed. After that a police force began to seem like a good idea, although anyone who has seen the police charging on horseback into a march might be feeling a bit confused at this point.

During 2008 and 2009 the relationship between police and protestors was tested to its utmost, and the resultant scandals have led to countless reviews and investigations. The two flash-points were Climate Camp 2008, where the Kent police spent £5.3m on a colossal stop and search operation and in the process confiscated as potential weapons balloons, colouring crayons and a clown outfit; and the G20 protests in London on April 1 2009, where police used the controversial "kettling" technique to tightly enclose protestors and keep them penned into specific areas.

Ian Tomlinson, a newspaper vendor who happened to be walking through the area, was violently pushed to the ground by police and later died. The incident was captured on videophone and made public, and the resulting furore will, observers hope, lead to serious reform of public order policing tactics. There are calls for a "human rights-based" approach to public policing, such as is practiced in Northern Ireland, where human rights observers work with police to make sure that policing accords with human rights standards. It's been noticeable that policing tactics since the G20 protests have been much more understated, and Climate Camp 2009, held on Blackheath in the south of London, was pretty much a police-free zone.

The Guardian: April 2 2009

All day long yesterday, the contrast between the two protests taking place in the City of London could not have been greater. Around the Bank of England where protestors were kettled by police the atmosphere was febrile, silent except for the clatter of the helicopters and the occasional rising chant: "Whose street? Our street!"

A few hundred feet down the road in Bishopsgate, however, it was a different story altogether, with music, drumming, dancing and face-painting. Climate Camp, having taken possession of this stretch of London road, proceeded to turn it into a mini-Glastonbury, complete with queues for the toilet and tent cities.

Which made it all the more shocking when, at 7.10pm, with no warning whatsoever, helmeted riot police suddenly marched towards the crowd and closed off the street.

Clamping together both ends of the protest simultaneously, they trapped several thousand people in the area, and used their batons in several places. "Why are they doing this?" said one of the Climate Camp legal observers who, like me, had ended up by chance on the outside of the kettle. "It's been completely peaceful all day long, there's no need for this at all."

In the scuffles that followed the police action at the Bank of England end where we stood, one policewoman was felled and had to be taken off for medical attention, while we witnessed several protestors being hit and kicked by police holding the line together.

The police slowly moved those outside the line back – using the same technique they had used by the Bank of England of kettling the central group and building up a large gap between them and any other protestors nearby.

Around 8 o'clock one protestor, Dave from South Africa, stumbled towards the group: he'd attempted to sneak round police lines and had, he said, been forced face down into the ground, and had his wrists bent as far forwards as they would go. In a clear state of shock he said: "The police told me that I was lucky they weren't breaking my wrists, that I would feel this for three days." On the left side of his face was a bleeding gash from contact with the road.

The police had initially indicated that they would start to let people out after a couple of hours, but as the night wore on there was no sign of that beginning, and no information from the police. Observers were increasingly worried about protestors with small children, and the growing cold.

But inside the kettle the mood was, apparently, not too bad. The Bicycology group carried on playing music, there was a bit of performance poetry, and more dancing. "About 11pm," said one protestor, Jenny Hill. "I started making a sandwich for a friend after the central kitchen had closed, and then discovered stashes of bread and peanut butter and jam, and ended up making about two hundred."

When the police finally began letting people out, at about 11.30pm, she was relieved to go home, but like other protestors could not understand the way police dealt with them. Another protestor recounts the way that police at the end forced them out without giving them time to get their tents or belongings, after holding them there for five hours. "It was all done in a mood of violence," she said. "It had been really peaceful all day, so I don't understand why it had to end like that."

So it was a long day with a fairly miserable ending. The legality of the kettle is under scrutiny, and Climate Camp are still going through the process of finding out if there were arrests. It was never going to be a beautiful sunset, but most people believe it could have ended very, very differently.

It's vital to know your rights during demonstrations, marches, civil disobedience and direct action. Firstly, it keeps you calmer. Secondly, it saves you from getting into daft arguments. I met one campaigner who didn't realise the police had the right to take her fingerprints in the police station and ended up having a big row after her arrest, which stressed her out even more. So what can the police do?

Under the Police and Criminal Evidence Act 1984, [or the Police Criminal Evidence (NI) Order 1989 in Northern Ireland] police have powers to stop and search you if they have reasonable grounds for suspicion that you have committed or are about to commit a crime. They can seize anything illegal that they find. If asked, they must tell you on what grounds they are searching you. "Reasonable grounds" means there must be some basis for the officer's belief that can be fairly evaluated by a third party – just a hunch or an instinct is not good enough. Under section 60 of the Criminal Justice Act a senior officer can grant a blanket order for an area which means that police operating there have the power to stop and search you for weapons and order you to take off a mask or anything else which might obscure your identity.

Police also have the power to search your home or office; contrary to all the films, they don't always need a search warrant, but they must have a good reason – for example, they must be coming in to arrest someone, or to save life or limb, or to prevent damage to property. In Northern Ireland recent changes to the law mean police have more license to grab documents and computer files and can hold them for up to 48 hours. They may search with your consent, in which case you need to give it in writing. If a policeman asks you to come down to the station to "help with enquiries", you can refuse.

You do not have to give your name when you have been stopped and questioned, or searched. The police can arrest you for this refusal if you are: driving a vehicle, or involved in some way in an accident; suspected of anti-social behaviour; or if they wish to summons you for an offence or issue a fixed penalty notice. (They can also arrest you for refusing to give your name and address if you're disrupting a lawful public meeting, under the Public Meeting Act 1908.)

When can they arrest you? When:
1. You have committed, are committing or are about to commit an offence (criminal damage, perhaps, or threatening behaviour, or simply obstructing the highway).

2. A police officer has reasonable grounds for suspecting that you have committed, are committing or are about to commit an offence.
3. A police officer has reasonable grounds to suspect you are guilty of an offence that he or she has reasonable grounds to suspect has been committed.

The arrest must also be deemed necessary – for example, because the police need your name and address and believe you have given them incorrect information, or because they want to prevent you causing physical injury or obstructing the highway.

Frankly, most things are covered in here, aren't they? The police can always come up with a reason for hauling you away if they want to. They must, however, inform you that they are arresting you as they do it. So, off you go into the van. At this point the police are not allowed to carry on questioning you until you get back to the police station, unless they think that some kind of harm to others, or to property, can be prevented by information that you hold, or that others may be alerted who are suspected of the offence but not yet arrested. If they want to question you, they need to caution you, otherwise your answers cannot be given as evidence in court.

Once you're in police custody you should be cautioned again, and then told of your rights: to have someone informed of your arrest, to have free independent legal advice (thanks, Magna Carta!), and to consult the policing codes of practice. You will also be shown your "custody record" and asked to sign it to say that you have been informed of the above rights. Any comments that you make will be noted on this custody record. If you ask for legal advice, the police cannot interview or continue to interview you until the solicitor arrives, unless they have the authority of an officer of superintendent rank or above.

The police can keep you for up to 36 hours without charging you, but the final 12 of those 36 must be authorised by an officer of superintendent rank or above. If authorised by a magistrate, you can be held for up to 96 hours without charge.

Once you are under arrest, the police don't need your permission to take fingerprints, photos, oral swabs, saliva or footwear impressions. They can use force if necessary. If you have been arrested but not charged, and the police suspect that misuse of a Class A drug led to your involvement in an offence, they may test you for that Class A drug. They need your permission, but it is an offence to refuse "without good cause". (The law is unspecific about what good cause might be.) They do need permission to take a blood sample, a urine sample, a semen sample, a dental impression, a pubic hair sample or a tissue sample.

What is the difference between the police taking you in, and actually charging you? Well, after questioning you and after investigation into how much evidence is available, the police will decide whether or not to charge you with an offence – they'll take advice on this from the Crown Prosecution Service (in England and Wales), the Crown Office (in Scotland) or the Public Prosecution Office (in Northern Ireland). They may, while deciding whether or not to charge you, impose pre-charge bail conditions upon you. These conditions are a fairly recent development, and can include being banned from going near power stations, airports, etc. They can also forbid contact with other activists.

If you are charged with an offence, this essentially means the courts will begin to wend their way to trial. Until the date of your first appearance in court, you may be granted police bail, or you may be remanded in custody. For the offences dealt with in this book, bail is the more likely option.

What are the alternatives to being charged? You could receive a caution (different from the type of caution talked about above) for which you would have to admit that you committed the offence and agree to receive the caution. There must also be some evidence that you committed the crime. The caution would go on the police database, but is not a criminal conviction and would not therefore form part of a permanent criminal record. It will, however, be on your record for a year after the end of the time it covered and if anyone – a potential employer for example – asks you if you've ever been cautioned you must answer honestly. Cautioning an offender is at the discretion of the police.

If arrested for breach of the peace – this is when your actions are likely to provoke someone else to violence, or cause harm to a person or a property – you could be brought before a magistrates court and "bound over to keep the peace". This is not a criminal conviction, just an undertaking to the court that you will not break the law for a specified period of time. Breach of the peace is a charge commonly made against protestors because it fufills the main priority of the police in a demonstration, which is to make sure that a protest is peaceful and carried out without interfering unduly with anyone's rights. If things get nasty, their duty is to break up the demonstration.

Failing to obey the order means you will have to pay a small fine, the amount of which will be specified at the time the bind-over order is made.

What impact does a criminal record have on your career? All convictions for which you receive a sentence of less than two-and-a-half years will eventually become "spent" (in seven to 10 years), which means that in due course you will not be obliged to disclose them to potential employers – and potential employers should not ask. There are exceptions to this, which relate mostly to work with vulnerable people.

In the meantime, it isn't impossible to get a job if you have a criminal record. The impact of your record will depend upon the offence you committed, the type of job you are applying for, and the attitude of your potential employer. If you are upfront about the nature of your offence, you may find that employers are quite willing to overlook it. Most will view a conviction stemming from non-violent protest as very difficult from one involving violence or dishonesty.

The Guardian: April 14 2009

As the police extend their operations to pre-emptive action (I expect Tom Cruise to come marching out at a police press conference anyday now, Minority Report pre-crime-style), another new police superpower needs to be watched carefully.

The boys in blue now have the power to decide pre-charge bail conditions, and slap them on just about anyone they want. This happened today to many of the protestors planning action on the Ratcliffe-on-Soar power station. They were arrested and, without being charged, had pre-bail conditions imposed on them that prevent them from approaching any power plant in the UK.

A limited form of this came along in the criminal justice bill in 2002, but the 2006 Police and Justice Act really went for it. Before this, police had been able to impose punitive bail conditions on you (forcing you to go somewhere or do something, rather than just report to the nearest police station) only if you had actually been charged with something. It was a tactic they used extensively at Newbury and still lob around with glee. A couple of years ago, for example, post-charge bail conditions were imposed on members of activist group Fit Watch which prevented them entering the M25 – the conditions were later struck down in court.

But under these new powers, before a single charge has been brought, the police have the right to impose conditions to make sure the person will be prevented from committing an offence while on bail, does not interfere with witnesses (so under those conditions you may be prevented from talking to your fellow activists or even friends), or will not otherwise obstruct the course of justice.

The potential for policing mischief here really is vast. In effect, it hands to the police powers that previously needed to be closely overseen by the entire legal system.

After all, what could be simpler? Swoop down on a group who you know to be associated with direct action, and impose pre-charge bail conditions on them which prevent them going near airports, or the City of London, or power stations, or anywhere you please, really. The bail conditions remain in place while the "investigation" continues, and there is no time limit (despite a standing committee recommendation that one should exist) on pre-charge bail conditions.

Even more worryingly, the current Home Office review of police legislation includes a proposal to make breaking your pre-charge bail conditions a criminal offence. At this point it all gets horrifyingly Alice in Wonderland, and into the realm, surely, of a world far, far beyond the Human Rights Act which promised us freedom of movement, freedom of association and thought. At least under the much-criticised Harassment Act (sorry, Protection from Harassment) a case needed to be made, legal procedure needed to be followed, you actually needed to be found guilty of something or other. Under this legislation, however, you can potentially be arrested and have pre-bail conditions set stating that, say, you are not allowed near an airport which would make going near an airport a criminal offence – without any proof of innocence or guilt having been offered at any point.

Chapter Six
Boycotts

Thousands of football supporters are rushing in a red and white torrent down the chute from Wembley tube station into the mouth of the new stadium. It's a mellow Saturday afternoon in September, and here and there in the crowd are flashes of blue: this afternoon's match pitches England (red and white) against Israel (blue and white) in a crucial qualifier for the European Championship.

On the right, about halfway to the stadium, 30 or so people are standing in a box of crowd-control barriers holding signs reading "Boycott Israeli Goods" and "Palestine Solidarity", with a line of police racked protectively in front of them. The chanting of the fans surging past drowns out most of their slogans, but as you get closer you can hear: "Palestine will be free, from the river to the sea."

The young man singing is enjoying himself, riffing the chant all over the place, and the protestors on either side of him are also smiling; it is a moment before I realise that the football supporters walking past are shouting "Fuck off home!" as the protestors' smiles get even wider. Some passersby nod, but most shout, make obscene gestures. One England fan starts screaming threats, and Israeli fans are incandescent. Two stretch out the Israeli flag in front of the protestors and literally dance with fury, while others walk over to grab the leaflets and tear them up, scattering the pieces theatrically.

The men and women of the Palestine Solidarity Campaign appear – fortunately – to thrive in the face of opposition. They don't, however, seem to be getting much support for their boycott from the crowd, or from the country as a whole. How many people in Britain are taking part in the Boycott Israeli Goods campaign? The organisers themselves have no idea, but I suspect the numbers are not enormous. Some of the trade unions have signed up, and a controversial vote in 2005 saw the Association of University Teachers pass a boycott of two Israeli universities. But many people have no idea the campaign exists, and when I ask friends – lefty friends, too – if they'd support a boycott on Israel the response is not necessarily positive: some say that they have some sympathy with the Israelis even if they disagree with Israel's treatment of the Palestinians. Others don't trust their own understanding of the situation in the Middle East: they worry that the media are distorting the picture so that they can no longer tell who is hurting who. "Besides," one tells me, "there are so many boycotts. I can't keep track."

Boycotts have always been troublesome as a tactic. Part of the problem arises, I think, because people misunderstand what you can do with them, what they're for, and try to use them in inappropriate situations. They come in a confusing variety, as well, with some boycotters attempting to financially damage their oppressors, such as the American colonists who refused to drink tea from the British East India Company, while others try to exert pressure on behalf of third parties, such as the Britons who stopped buying sugar in opposition to the slave trade. And, often, their visibility bears no relation to their effectiveness.

Throughout the 17th century, for example, the Quakers (who deserve a book to themselves when it comes to protesting) had been trying to get people interested in the evil of slavery. They faced an almost impossible task for two reasons: firstly, slavery underpinned the British economy and so had very powerful friends, and secondly, they were Quakers and as such not permitted to be MPs or make too much noise in public, the British people being incredibly suspicious of any kind of "outsider". But slowly they managed to gather other allies: the self-trained lawyer Granville Sharp, who tried to get rid of slavery through the courts, the former slave Olaudah Equiano, whose book about his experiences is still in print today, the larger-than-life Thomas Clarkson, who travelled all over England and went to France too in the service of the cause, the MP William Wilberforce, who was their man in parliament, and last of all the legal master-mind James Stephen, who finally came up with a way of tricking the Foreign Slave Trade Act through in 1807.

The abolition campaign was something completely new. It asked people who were still arguing about their own rights to recognise the rights of Africans, who were regarded by many as an entirely subordinate race. It required its supporters to do something that is still difficult today – to make the leap of imagination into someone else's life, and act on their behalf. The climate change campaign faces this difficulty: at the moment if you live in the UK or the US you are campaigning either on behalf of people far away who are suffering the effects now, or on behalf of yourself 20 years in the future. (A few more fires in California or hurricanes in Birmingham will bring the realities a little closer, but ideally the campaign would like to get ahead of the weather.)

Why I fight

Andrew Sharp

Has raised public awareness of small farmers and rare breed cattle

I grew up on farms. My dad's farm, my uncle's farm: farming goes back generations and generations in my family. I would have been a farmer myself, but my half-brother got our father's place. I became a butcher instead, doing an apprenticeship at 14 and then opening up my own outfit when I was 19. I thought I could do everything.

We've always farmed Herdwick sheep up in the Lake District, so that was what I was selling, and back home no one would even bother to ask. But when I started up a stall in Borough food market in London, customers kept asking me what kind of sheep this was, so I realised that elsewhere people were really interested. I'd always had the links with the local farmers, but now we formalised everything and called ourselves a cooperative, because we realised that if people understood where the meat was coming from we'd be able to get the premium we needed. I'm a good Lancastrian, but London is the centre for making things happen, and Borough market is the food centre of London: you never know who you might be talking to when you're behind the stall. You can educate people and influence them, and really get the word out.

It's hard to make a living as a hill farmer, but hill farming is something you do because it's in your blood. How can you measure the economic value of managing the Lake District? Do people realise when they're walking through these hills that the paths, the landscape would be completely different without the sheep? Are these sheep just food producers, or are they the guardians and lawnmowers of the countryside? You can't modernise hill farming: you can't speed up the sheep. But it's the lungs of England.

In the 1780s the abolition campaign took off like a rocket, thanks to the emergence of a middle class with slightly more time to worry about other people, and the growing political consciousness of the working class. Petitions in support of the committee of abolitionists were signed everywhere, and huge crowds gathered to hear Clarkson speak. But, as Adam Hochschild describes in his book Bury the Chains: "most dramatic was the contagious spread of a new tactic the committee itself had never considered ... From the Plymley household in the west to the North Sea, from Josiah Wedgwood's home in the Midlands to the highlands of Scotland, hundred of thousands of people had stopped using sugar." Wilberforce, who was essentially conservative, suffered the same anxieties over the boycott as Martin Luther King would two centuries later during the Montgomery bus boycott, but Clarkson was over the moon about it all, recounting joyfully that "there was no town through which I passed in which there was not some individual who had left off the use of sugar ... They were from all ranks and parties. Rich and poor, churchmen and dissenters ... Even grocers had left off trading in the article." Hochschild quotes one of the contemporary pamphlets that urged the boycott: "As he sweetens his tea, let him say as he truly may, this lump cost the poor slave a groan, and this a bloody stroke with the cartwhip."

It's a bit chicken and egg, but I think it's worth arguing that the boycott – getting the sugar to embody the pain and suffering of the slaves – brought the reality of slavery into the homes of British people. Hochschild suggests that support sprang from long experience of the press gangs that roved the country snatching men off the streets whenever ships' crews needed replenishing, and that must have played a part. But the boycott also forged an imaginative connection between the kitchen of a Briton and a slave plantation thousands of miles away, empowering women in particular (who tended to lead the campaign) to do things in their own homes that might have a political impact beyond. It taught the idea of solidarity and DIY politics – it was a mini political education all by itself.

However, the boycott had absolutely no impact in achieving the abolitionists' ultimate aims: the Foreign Slave Trade Act that outlawed the slave trade in the British empire did not come for another two decades, while slavery itself was wiped out very slowly, country by country, over the following century. The US only abolished the practice in 1865, after the American civil war.

Let's jump forward to 1880, during what was known as the land war in Ireland, when the Irish National Land League began its campaign for the three Fs: "fair rent, fixity of tenure and free sale". Trying to avoid the violence that was surging around the country, the Land League persuaded members to target an English land agent called Captain Charles C Boycott; when local peasants refused to bring in his harvests, deliver his post or serve him in shops, the government was forced to send in the troops to do the farm work. As Boycott chucked it all in and went back to England, the use of the tactic to which he has given his name spread, and after several months of serious unrest the authorities came up with the Land Act, which may not have solved everything but was certainly a concession.

This time around, in other words, a boycott actually succeeded in achieving its aim. But this is what I mean by troublesome. What, exactly, can a boycott do?

Mark Farmaner is king of the modern-day boycott. He started his political life as a teenager on the picket line outside South Africa House in London, worked for Christian Aid and the Jubilee debt-relief campaign, and now heads the Burma Campaign. I go to see him in autumn 2007, as the world watches thousands of monks lead protests through the streets of Rangoon. His eyes are bloodshot and he looks slightly delirious with tiredness. All the same he is wonderful, bracing company, with a refreshingly pragmatic approach to campaigning.

Farmaner uses the boycott like a dagger. He has "persuaded" at least eight companies, among them British American Tobacco, Kookai, Mark One and Triumph, to pull out of Burma, and he does this by being extremely focused. "The first thing we do when we're considering a boycott is very detailed research into the company to find its weak points and strengths, and to look for potential pressure points," he says. "Are the media going to be interested? Do they have shareholders? Do they have investors? If they're a global concern, you're going to need to put an international campaign into place because if they're just being boycotted in one city they're not going to care. We decided not to look at companies which deal mainly with other businesses, rather than the public, as in the end we thought we wouldn't be able to apply enough pressure to them." The boycott, for Farmaner, is not used as a broad tool against Burma, but specifically against individual companies, as part of a range of tactics in what he calls a "mosquito strategy". This is when boycotts really function.

He suggests the campaign group "should have something planned every week for the first six months of the boycott: postcards, protests, handing letters to staff as they go into the office". For the campaign to get British American Tobacco out of Burma, he and his colleagues found out the names and home addresses of all the directors and sent press cuttings about the regime to their homes. If you can get some big colourful coup in there too, you're on to a winner: when the Burma Campaign targeted the lingerie-maker Triumph, they had posters of women in barbed wire bras, which was, Farmaner thinks, "the only campaign I've ever run which made it into the Sun". And once you get a reputation, just the threat can be enough. Mark One pulled out four hours after Farmaner sent out the press releases. It helps, he points out, if companies actually know they're being targeted. "I get so many things asking me to boycott someone, but not asking me to contact the company and tell them. How are they going to know? Where does the pressure come from?"

The sharp-eyed reader will point out, however, that Farmaner has only achieved his short-term goals – getting a handful of companies out of Burma. In terms of the bigger aim – regime change – it could be argued that the boycotts don't even make a dent. They are perhaps just making poor people poorer while the country's military rulers carry on stuffing their pockets. Farmaner agrees this is a problem, but says: "Our mandate to work on Burma comes from the democracy movement in Burma, and they are the ones who decide." In other words, the Burma Campaign is not just a bunch of middle-class first-worlders Doing Good; it works on behalf of the Burmese people – and they, I should think, can make their own minds up.

So, in short, if you are using a boycott towards a big strategic aim – ending an oppressive regime, say – so far it seems that the most you are likely to achieve is to get people feeling solidarity with mistreated people on the other side of the world (although that's not necessarily something to be sniffed at). Although the South African boycott ran for more than 30 years, I have not been able to track down any record of the authorities in Pretoria angsting about it and wondering if perhaps they should pay attention and start dismantling apartheid. Governments don't really feel the financial pressure (unless you're organising a really huge refusal to pay tax, which actually would fall more into the category of civil disobedience).

If, however, you are using boycotts for tactical purposes – to get a company to stop doing something for example – you do have a chance of changing behaviour, because they really are vulnerable to both the financial pressure and to What The Customer Thinks. (The American campaigner Ralph Nader estimated that a company would only want to see its sales go down about 2–3 per cent before it took action.) The most famous and effective consumer boycott was against Shell, when plans to dump the Brent Spar oil storage buoy at sea were made public by Greenpeace. Thousands spontaneously boycotted Shell's petrol stations, and the oil company backed down within a few weeks.

Do what Farmaner says – target a specific company, do your research, keep up the pressure, get the word out, make your supporters write to the firm, get it in the press and keep going until the company gives in. Don't, however cross you may feel after reading the newspaper that morning, just launch your boycott out into the sky with no follow-up or back-up planned. You just muddy the waters for the guys who are doing this seriously.

Ethical shopping

Interestingly, the recession has not brought catastrophe to the growing number of designers, retailers and farmers who are trying to make their living "ethically". Doomsayers who feared that the whole movement, still so young and fragile, would be drowned beneath the tsunami of the banking crisis, have been proved wrong, and although things are tough, most people are optimistic.

The idea of using your spending power to make a statement about your beliefs obviously goes back a long way, as we have seen. But in the 80s and 90s it began to be formalised into a movement. The "100percenters", as they sometimes call themselves, are the original pioneers of Fairtrade; they opened up individual shops, set up close relationships with weavers or potmakers in developing countries, and tried to get them a good deal here. But Oxfam and Christian Aid both wanted to take this further; the result, in 1994, was the Fairtrade Foundation.

Fifteen years down the line, it's possible to see what a huge impact this innovation has had. The figures alone tell the story: in 1994 the total annual sales of Fairtrade coffee were £2.2m; in 2008 they were £137.3m; in 2000, the first year that Fairtrade bananas went on sale, annual sales were £7.8m; by 2008 they had risen to £184m. The total annual sales of Fairtrade goods in 1994 was £2.7m; by 2008 that had ballooned to a staggering £712.6m. And numbers have not dropped in the recession – in fact for Fairtrade and the Marine Stewardship Council (see page 64) they've continued to rise, suggesting that when we're a bit hard-up it's even more important to us that the family who picked the coffee beans for our morning java are not living in penury.

But does ethical shopping work? Rob Harrison, a dry sort of bloke with a certain vocal resemblance to John Peel, was one of the founders of Ethical Consumer magazine back in the 90s. He'd been interested in the potential of consumer action for some time, had grown up with the anti-apartheid boycott in the background, but was only finally convinced of the possibilities in 1986, when Barclays Bank unexpectedly pulled out of South Africa. "I think the Barclays decision was a bit of a personal moment for me," he says. "It was always used as an example in the 70s of why boycotts were useless, and then suddenly Barclays did a complete U-turn."

Helpfully, the anti-apartheid movement had leaked an internal memo in which Barclays admitted that "our customer base was beginning to be affected". It turned out that, after a good few years of hearing about Barclays' involvement in South Africa, British students had stopped opening accounts with the bank, whose share of the student market had fallen from 27 per cent to 17 per cent. Harrison saw the light.

Ethical Consumer magazine is the result: a hard-working, thoroughly decent research centre that tries to impose some kind of transparency on to multinational corporations, while at the same time giving customers hard-to-get information about a company's environmental policy, its treatment of unions, the amount of money it gives to charity and more. It's not a glamorous magazine. In fact it's the anti-glamour of the magazine world, although the covers have got a bit jauntier recently. The letters pages are perfect microcosms of the life of the ethical consumer, agonising over the most minuscule shadings of grey – if this publisher has also published a book containing an ad for a company that used to work in Burma, should I, I dunno, read their books? The reviews – of campingware, or school uniforms, or yoghurts – are painstaking and extremely useful. The sudden trendiness of things ethical or green has slightly bypassed the magazine, which is probably a good thing: instead it remains a solid, stoical part of the green movement, having a bit of a laugh and a bit of a poke at corporations, and generally chugging along.

There is, however, a growing group, spearheaded by environmental campaigners such as George Monbiot, who believe that "green consumerism is another form of atomisation – a substitute for collective action. No political challenge can be met by shopping." It is undoubtedly true that consumption gone crazy, our church of retail, is what causes a great number of this planet's woes. But we do still need to eat, to clothe ourselves, to have shelter. I'm not suggesting buying some of the extraneous "green" gadgets that increasingly clog up the airways, but can we use our money to do good? Harrison believes that we can, and points to the free-range egg as an example, an item that has increasingly become an everyday part of shopping. Normal, non-campaigning consumers (I hate being called a consumer – it always makes me feel like some kind of Pac-Man – so I apologise for using the term here) are thinking greener, the ethical finance market is booming (worth something like £11bn in the UK in 2006), ethical fashion is a must, darling, it's all go on hemp and recycled bottles … It's not the answer to anything, but Ralph Nader expresses it well: "The possibility that consumers banding together can muster their organised intelligence to play a major role in shaping economic policy and the future of our political economy is an unsettling one for the megacorporations that play much of the world's economy."

So what's the best way to use your money for the greater good? My grandfather used to quote William Morris: "Have nothing in your house that you do not know to be useful or believe to be beautiful." It's a basic rule for shopping of any kind, but particularly ethical shopping: don't go out and buy things just because they're green, or Fairtrade – buy them because you need them to live. And, very occasionally, because you find them beautiful. So don't buy bags of organic oranges and then forget to eat them – better not to have bought them in the first place. If you run out of paper, that is the time to buy a nifty notebook of sheep poo paper, and not a second before. If summer is coming and your T-shirts have all been eaten by the moths, than that's the moment to buy that organic cotton fairtrade I Love Africa sweatshirt, when it will actually form a functional part of your wardrobe instead of another add-on. The best kind of ethical products – such as an ethical bank account, green electricity, a vegetable box from a local farm, free-range eggs rather than battery, Fairtrade coffee – are part of your life, not just something you've bought as a one-off.

Fairtrade is not the only "ethical" shopping label out there. You can also look out for:

The Forestry Stewardship Council: The FSC mark indicates that a piece of wood has come from a sustainably grown source, rather than say, an illegal logging operation in a rainforest.

Organic: Organic farming uses little or no chemical fertiliser, herbicides and pesticides, so consuming organically means that the carbon footprint of your food is far smaller, as the production of these chemicals is very carbon-intensive. The animal welfare standards are also better than under intensive farming. The Soil Association is the major UK body that certifies organic products; it's known to have some of the strictest criteria around. There are other certifying bodies recognised by the government, however, such as the Organic Food Federation, Organic Farmers and Growers, Demeter (for biodynamic products), and the Scottish Organic Producers Association.

Freedom Food: The RSPCA award this label to farms which meet its animal welfare standards.

The Marine Stewardship Council: Motivated by rising anxiety about the condition (near extinction in some cases) of the world's fish stocks, the MSC has been inspecting fisheries for ten years now to make sure that the fishermen are working sustainably. If they are satisfied the fishery is certified and allowed to show the little blue tick on their fish; watch out for it next time you go shopping. It's easier and easier to find as the MSC is growing rapidly: by 2009, 12 per cent of the world's wild fish harvest destined for human consumption was either certified or undergoing the process of certification.

But, it must be said, labelling is a minefield. What does "outdoor-reared" mean on your packet of pork sausages? There's no recognised scheme for this bit of wordmanship: it can just mean that the pig spent a couple of months in the open air before being ushered back into the barn. Your best bet is either to buy foods labelled in a way that is clear, or to buy from small producers and retailers that know their stuff and can tell you all you need to know. As for clothes, a lot of the big retailers have signed up to the Ethical Trading Initiative, but that is basically a promise to try to do better, and not much more. Labour Behind the Label (you'll find all the necessary contact details at the end of this book) produces information about the approach that various chains are taking to their manufacturing process – this can be more useful. It's also worth visiting the Ecolabelling website, which contains information on eco-labels throughout the world. You need all the information you can get your hands on.

Chapter Seven
Letters

Letter-writing seems somehow old-fashioned. What, just pick up a pen (or keyboard) and write to the person you're unhappy with? But it is one of the simplest and most effective methods there is. It is, after all, the simple act of communicating your views to your target, and that must be at the heart of any successful campaign. No one can change if they are not sure what is required of them, and some of the most experienced campaigners, including Benedict Southworth, who heads the World Development Movement, name letter-writing as their favourite tactic. In the States the letter-writing party is a campaign staple, from the Bay Area Vegetarians who meet every month in Pizza Plaza, to Quaker groups setting up a letter-writing table after every week's service.

I think letter-writing can seem unlikely as a successful tactic because our society is so atomised. We see CEOs and MPs on television every day but we're far less likely to meet these people ourselves. But that's precisely why politicians and businesspeople respond so well to letters: you are a potential voter, or shopper, or investor, and your letter contains extremely useful information for them.

Take corporations: writing a **letter of complaint** to a company may seem like just a drop in the ocean, but if you approach it systematically, and if you're prepared to really enter into correspondence, you can achieve more than you would expect. Jasper Griegson, who as the Daily Express's "Complainer" spent many years extracting cheques and apologies from corporations on behalf of his readers, believes that companies "actually like complaints because complaints supply them with valuable feedback that otherwise they would only get by paying. Complaining is a bit like voting. By complaining you are exercising an important democratic right. It is not good enough or fair for you to slag off a company in the abstract if you have not given to those concerned your views on the subject that is eating you."

This idea of taking personal responsibility for making your views known to a corporation is firmly embedded in the consumer revolution that began at the end of the 19th century as shopping became institutionalised and the chain store was invented. By the 1920s, with consumption soaring, there was a growing awareness of the possibility of being ripped off by large, increasingly anonymous companies. In the States a book called Your Money's Worth was published in 1927, and a year later one of its authors founded the consumer rights group Consumers Inc. The whole idea of consumer awareness was just getting established when it was banjaxed by the Depression and the second world war.

What with poverty, rationing, austerity, mass fatalities and so on, it was a while before society could again whip up much interest in issues such as value for money or after-sales service. And then, in the mid 1950s, a young woman living in London called Dorothy Goodman wanted to buy a steam iron and have central heating installed but couldn't find any advice on what would be best. She set up a small group, which began to test things out; the result was the Consumers' Association, and Which? magazine. The association's first breakthroughs included the revelation that all the various kinds of aspirin on the market contained the same ingredients and customers should just buy the cheapest, and the fact that orange drink, by law, did not have to contain any oranges.

In his essay, A Brief History of Consumer Activism, Tim Lang argues that the consumer champion Ralph Nader, whose 1965 book Unsafe at Any Speed exposed the car industry's neglect of safety issues, was then part of a new wave of consumer awareness calling for corporate responsibility. Alternatively, you can see Nader as a kind of logical next step from the housewives of Which?. Sure, the housewives don't have the same kind of firebrand glamour, but it's hard not to respect them all the same – so practical, so Marks & Sparks, and yet so utterly remorseless. The modern anti-capitalists – though they'd hate it if you told them so – are really the heirs of both these schools of consumer awareness.

But whether you're contacting a corporation out of concern over their human rights record, or to complain about a defective condom, the technique is identical. Anna Tims, the Guardian's consumer champion, says that it's vital to be polite and reasonable, because otherwise you increase the chance that your letter will just be ignored. "Even I'm tempted to ditch letters from people who are just ranting, so imagine how a company feels."

Why I fight

Dave Webb
Yorkshire convener with the Campaign for Nuclear Disarmament

About 25 years ago I did a PhD in space physics and then got a job with the Ministry of Defence. I worked for the directorate of scientific intelligence, and my job entailed monitoring the space activities of the Soviet Union. I justified it by telling myself that I wasn't actually building any nasty weapons, but after a while I realised that I was supplying information that would lead to a heightening of the technological arms race.

So I left and got a job at Leeds Polytechnic teaching engineering, and joined CND. I'd never really joined anything before, even though back when I was a student there had been marches every day. But now it felt like the best way of changing things. There have been some difficult times, when only four or five people turned up and you're standing round on the corner of the

---

street getting wet. But I've met some really committed, wonderful people from all around the world who belong to the movement.

There are people in China and Iran who try to get information about what's going on out to us. They want to change things and sometimes that can end up in tragic circumstances. I now teach a peace and conflict resolution MA at Leeds: we teach students different ways of researching information, different ways of resolving situations. I don't know where that will take our students because it's a new course.

But this is what it's about: if you're not happy with the way things are, then you've got to try to find some way to change them. I came to believe that the only way to do it was through this sort of massive grassroots movement. I believe that CND has had some successes over the years, although of course we haven't got rid of nuclear weapons. But I think it's due to the peace movement, and the fact that we tried to make clear the horrors that a nuclear war would bring, that there hasn't been a nuclear war.

The first thing to do is **work out who you should be writing to**. "Find out people's names – that gives your letter more impact." Follow all the old-fashioned rules of letter-writing, rather than doing it email-style (snail mail is better than email, she believes, because "you never really know where those emails go"). So begin your letter Dear so-and-so, and put your address at the top and your name clearly at the bottom beneath your signature. Remember, they can't respond to you if they don't have your address. Tims says she's astonished at how often people don't follow these basic rules. Keep a copy for yourself, and start a log of letters and phone calls, with dates and times and names and as much as you can remember of each conversation.

It's also worth sending your letter to multiple destinations: find out the name of a couple of the directors and cc your complaint to them, as well as the complaints or customer relations department or whoever you're targeting. In Griegson's book The Complete Complainer he gives an example of contacting three directors of the same company in this way: one did not respond, one offered a partial refund, and the third offered a full refund. You could also find out if your target is subject to any kind of regulator – Ofcom, Ofgem, Ofwat, Ofsted, the Financial Services Authority, the Advertising Standards Authority, Postcomm, the Office of Rail Regulation, the Civil Aviation Authority, the Office of Fair Trading, the Food Standards Agency, etc. Writing to the regulator as well will mean that your complaint is logged; if there are enough complaints, at some point it may even trigger an enquiry (it was mounting complaints that led to Ofcom's 2007 investigation into the way mobile phone contracts are sold). If you have concerns about politics, human rights, working practices or instances of discrimination, it might be worth looking through the Organisation for Economic Co-operation and Development guidelines on how corporations should operate. If you think the company might be in breach of the guidelines you can refer the matter to the "national contact point", whose work is outlined in chapter 13, Legal action.

As for politicians, MPs do pay attention to the letters they receive, and will almost always answer. They even take note of those preprinted **postcards** that campaigns ask their supporters to send in, and, according to one parliamentary researcher, start to think about taking some kind of action when they've got a stack that's about a thumbnail's width. There is a wonderful website called Write to Them (details at the end of the book) that takes all the faff out of contacting your MP, and will tell you who he or she is if you're not entirely sure. You can knock off an email in 10 minutes, which is very satisfying and worthwhile (although obviously if you start emailing every day your MP may think you're a stalker). Again, keep your letter polite: a rude rant about Palestine will simply be ignored, but if you engage with your MP and show some awareness of their own position on the subject, they will respond and perhaps be moved to take the matter further. And if you write to them a couple of times and establish a relationship, you're on the road towards lobbying, more of which in the next chapter. Local councils are also keen on getting letters – they are close to their constituents, and information from the public is very useful to them.

The **letters page in a newspaper** is also a fantastic forum for local and national issues; when I worked at a local London paper called the Camden New Journal in the 90s we gave over two whole pages to letters every week, and still had far more than we could print. Rows about parking restrictions, council housing, licensing laws, policing levels went on from week to week and were read avidly by the local council (who actually tried to ban the Journal from the town hall at one point – presumably because they were so fed up with being slagged off in it). Maybe you've never even glanced at the letters pages in your newspaper, but lots of people read them intensively, and carry on energetic and angry debates through them. Bertrand Russell, philosopher and anti-nuclear campaigner, wrote hundreds of letters to editors, and it was an angry letter from a reader to the Times in 1937 that led to the creation of the 999 service. It's a tribute to their power that in 2005 Labour press officers in the national office adopted the practice known as "astroturfing" – simulating grassroots support – by writing model letters for supporters and party members to send to local papers.

Letters can also have a huge impact internationally, as the work of Amnesty over the years has shown. James Savage, head of letter-writing campaigns there, sent out an alert in 2005 about Mohammed Abbou, a Tunisian lawyer who had been imprisoned after working on human rights cases and publishing articles that were critical of his government. In an interview after his early release in 2007, Abbou said that the support "was of invaluable help to me and especially to my family. I wasn't certain of getting out before the end [of my sentence] ... I would also like to say how touched I was to receive letters from seven- and eight-year-old children who wrote to me on behalf of Amnesty International Belgium. I had those letters read to my children."

All you need is a pen, a piece of paper, an envelope, and a stamp. You have to admit that there's a certain poetry to the endeavour.

The law and ... letter-writing

If you're planning to write a very full-on letter, make sure you read the notes about defamation on page 121.

You should also be aware of the Malicious Communications Act 1988, which makes it an offence to send something "of an indecent or grossly offensive nature" with the intention of causing distress or anxiety. A number of a pro-life campaigners, for example, have been prosecuted for sending letters containing photographs of aborted foetuses. The maximum sentence under the act is six months in prison. And under the Criminal Justice Police Act 2001 this section has been extended to cover not just letters but also sending electronic communications and "any article".

Chapter Eight
Lobbying parliament

Lobbying is one of the eternals of politics. You can't credit anyone with inventing the idea, as people have leaned on politicians and asked them favours and made "helpful" suggestions since time immemorial. But it would be rude not to mention Francis Place, a self-educated tailor with 15 children, who brought extraordinary powers of organisation to grassroots politics just as the clamour for suffrage was beginning to get louder and louder. In 1807 the radical Francis Burdett won his seat in the House of Commons in large part owing to Place's zeal for organising. Place, a leading member of the Westminster Committee, which was campaigning on Burdett's behalf, is described by the historian EP Thompson as working "for three weeks without payment, from dawn until midnight, keeping careful accounts, collating canvass returns, and preparing reports for the general committee".

Thompson called Place "an organiser of genius", and a few years later Place would turn that genius to use again with a successful campaign to repeal the Combination Acts that had in effect made trade unions illegal. His National Political Union (founded in 1830) was one of the first leftwing lobbying groups in existence. This was the moment, after the political agony and ecstasy of the 1790s, when people from outside the MP class – ie, who didn't own 10,000 acres of land – began to take seriously the possibility of participating in politics.

It wasn't until 1926, however, that the UK's first professional political lobbying company was set up by Commander Christopher Powell, who had served in the Royal Navy, and Charles Watney, who had previously been the political correspondent for the News Chronicle. Watney would famously go down to the House of Commons with that day's brief inside his top hat.

All around Watney and Powell the public relations industry was coming to life: Editorial Services, one of the very first PR firms, had been set up by their colleague Sir Basil Clarke just four years earlier, and other firms were popping up everywhere you looked. It was the obvious step, really: as newspapers, books and radio penetrated a growing number of homes, the necessity of managing the messages and the media became increasingly apparent. Public interest groups and businesses then began to wonder if they should not also be paying people to make sure their interests were represented to the government. The steady rise of Labour only confirmed big business in this relatively new political party's determination to make its case explicitly. A report by the Hansard Society in 2007 estimated that there are now at least 14,000 people involved in PR related to public affairs, and probably significantly more.

This is generally not seen as a very happy situation – in terms of public trust, lobbyists are right up there with journalists. One American lobbyist said: "My mother has never introduced me to her friends as 'my son, the lobbyist'. 'My son, the Washington representative', maybe. Or 'the legislative consultant'. Or 'the government relations counsel'. But never as a lobbyist. I can't say I blame her." Winston Churchill described them as "touts": The Labour MP Jon Trickett says he avoids them – "the professional ones, anyway" – like the plague. And there are pretty good reasons to hold them at arm's length: over the past few years some of our juiciest news stories have included lobbyists. In 1996, in the famous cash-for-questions saga, the Guardian alleged that one of the country's best-established lobbyists, Ian Greer, had bribed two Conservative MPs to ask questions on behalf of one of his clients. (Greer sued the Guardian for libel, but dropped his libel action before the end of the year.) A couple of years later Lobbygate lost lobbyist Derek Draper his job after he told an undercover journalist: "There are 17 people who count in this government. And to say I am intimate with every one of them is the understatement of the century."

The best-known lobby firms these days, such as Weber Shandwick (whose clients include General Motors, American Airlines, Electrolux and Microsoft), Grayling (Roche, Bayer, British Airways) and Bell Pottinger (BAE Systems, which must be a particularly juicy client) tend not to have the word "lobby" anywhere on their websites. The preferred terms include "public affairs" and "advocacy". Big business has the money to buy all the lobbying it needs, so a company such as BAE Systems, the third-largest global "defence" company with annual sales of over £15bn, can afford to pay specialists to follow every single full stop in the House of Commons that might affect it, all the research anyone might need, and the odd party too. The parliamentary researcher William Moy points out that big companies also have the ability to go direct to government departments and get a hearing; that's where most decisions are made. "And big business isn't the only group with a financial advantage. There are 679 charities with incomes over £10m, and they have as much money as the other 169,000 charities put together. Some public-sector organisations can spend a small fortune on lobbying, too. The way rich groups lobby can be very different from an ordinary person's or small charity's letter to an MP: glossy reports, sophisticated parliamentary monitoring, receptions in parliament and stands at party conferences. These cost thousands of pounds apiece," says Moy. And what can your grassroots campaign afford?

Well, before you fall sobbing on the floor, pull yourself together. Yes, it's unfair that the big guys have so much money, but that does not mean that the whole system of lobbying is evil. I think it's a vital part of the democratic system, and even businesses have the right to put their case to politicians. A study of MPs' receptiveness to lobbying revealed that they are far more likely to listen to what a charity is talking about than a business, so we should perhaps give MPs a small amount of credit for filtering some stuff. Which is all the more reason for us all to become lobbyists and put the other side. This afternoon!

Lobbying does not have to be left to paid specialists: it's very simple and absolutely anyone with reasonably good manners can do it. You need to do four things:

1. **Work out if going to the government is any use**: do you really want to be approaching a corporation, perhaps, and tailoring your campaign accordingly? If your concern is local, similarly, there's probably not much point in heading straight for the House of Commons, the Welsh Assembly, the Northern Ireland Assembly or the Scottish Parliament.

2. **You need to start finding your way around**. Let's begin in the House of Commons, with its 646 MPs, each of whom represents a constituency and has an office both there and in the House. You can find out more about them and their interests at the excellent website They Work for You (see the back of this book for details). The Guardian also has biographies of each MP on its website, along with contact information.

   Banked all around the House of Commons are government departments headed by ministers and staffed by civil servants. These are watched over by select committees made up of MPs – so the culture, media and sport committee, for example, keeps an eye on the administration, expenditure and policy of the department for culture, media and sport. There are also public bill committees, which are assigned to watch over upcoming bills, and joint committees that work with the House of Lords. All of these provide points of entry for the resourceful lobbyist. There are similar chinks and opportunities to be found at the Welsh Assembly, the Northern Ireland Assembly and the Scottish Parliament.

   To start making head and tail of all this, the best thing is to go to a few debates and committee meetings. These are usually open to the public. I've been to a couple in the Commons, and although these were not the most thrilling hours of my life, I came away with some new respect for MPs, who actually seem to work fairly hard. They are not, after all, busy taking bungs in brown envelopes. I also felt much less nervous about approaching them. They are, it turns out, human, doing basic, day-to-day stuff that keeps the country ticking over. The ones I've spoken to sometimes even appear to have a sense of humour. (They will, of course, probably lose it long before they reach ministerial level, but there you go …)

3. **You need to figure out who in this place will be interested in your issue**. Find out who is on the committee for the department that would cover it, and also take a look at the all-party groups (APGs), known as cross-party groups in Scotland and Wales and all-party interest groups in Northern Ireland. These are clubs of parliamentary representatives who are interested in specific issues; in the House of Commons there are APGs on every subject you can possibly imagine, from the aluminium industry to zoos and aquaria, and there is almost certainly one dealing with your area. If you have the strength, you can go through MPs' details on the website They Work for You: their biographies will give you an idea of their main interests. It's worth doing some research into the House of Lords: this is where many professional lobbyists head when they want an amendment to legislation. In the Commons, an amendment is discussed only if selected by the Speaker or the chairman of the public bill committee. In the Lords, any peer can table an amendment and every amendment is discussed and, if the peer wishes, voted on. So if you can get a peer on your side he or she can be very useful.

You've got your names. Now make a nice neat list. Neat is important, because you're going to be referring to this over and over again.

4. **The most nerve-racking step is to start contacting them**. What? What? But what should I say? Well, dear, that depends on

what you're contacting them about, doesn't it? Say, for example, you've formed a campaign group with the aim of getting the government to bring in carbon rationing. You've got a long list of MPs from the environment select committee, the environmental audit committee, the trade and industry select committee, the draft climate change bill joint committee, the climate change APG, and anyone you've come across who has ever asked a question about carbon rationing. You might start with a polite letter asking whether they have considered urging the government to make carbon rationing part of its climate change strategy. You can do this as a letter (either by snail mail or via the Write to Them website) from the campaign group, or you can all send individual ones if you feel like it. While you wait to hear back from the MPs, you could gather information about carbon rationing that might be of interest to them. Has anyone done any research into the practicalities, for example? Does anyone know how much it would cost to implement? Has anyone conducted a poll on how the general population feels about such an idea?

Why I fight

Kate Fowler
Animal rights campaigner

I've cared about animals for as long as I can remember. I grew up in Hertfordshire, in a small town on the edge of the countryside. I would get upset if a moth got caught in the washing-up bowl, or if I found an insect crushed in the garden. My aunt married a farmer, and we used to go and visit her in Devon for holidays, and it seemed absolutely perfect. It was only as I got older that I began to realise that all these cows and pigs were being turned into food: that the ones you got to know on one visit wouldn't be there on the next.

When I was eight years old I did a Save the Seal sponsored bike ride. I also used to go carol-singing – I'd drag my friends along – to raise money for animal rights organisations, and I can't imagine how it sounded, because I'm a terrible singer. It used to really upset me when people said "How do I know this will really go to charity?" because I was so passionate about it and shocked that they didn't believe me.

I was vegetarian by the age of 12, but didn't actually meet another vegetarian until I started university. When I got there I joined an animal welfare group, and within a couple of weeks was running it, because otherwise it was just going to fall apart. I didn't really want to do this for a living – I battled it for a while, because I'd like to have had an easy life doing something that didn't cause emotional upset every day of my life. I've worked at Viva, Peta and now Animal Aid. Some people cope by immersing themselves in the horror, others by just switching off; I need to balance it by spending time with my friends, who are all vegan too, and the animals I've rescued. We've achieved a lot in the last few years – the ban on battery cages that the European Union is bringing in, the ban on testing finished cosmetic products on animals – but it can never be enough and it can never be fast enough. Animals have the right to a life free from pain, free from human interference.

When they write back and say blah blah how interested they were to receive your letter, don't know anything about carbon rationing but will certainly bear it in mind, write to them again with this new information. Ask if they were aware of any of it. Enter into a correspondence with them: MPs genuinely take notice of the mail they get, as it is one of the best ways they have of knowing what people are interested in. They are more likely to answer if you actually live in their constituency and therefore represent a possible vote, but they tend to be reasonably good at replying to all mail: it's a very important part of their job. Perhaps one MP will be particularly interested in your idea, and write back at length, or even phone for a chat. He (or she, although given the lack of women MPs, it's more likely to be a he) may even suggest taking it further. Remember that once you have reached a politician, your journey doesn't end there. You can't just hand your problem over to your MP and expect them to sort it out for you: you need to perceive them as a tool to help, and carry on piling on the pressure from every possible angle.

Hang on, hang on, you say: this is all very well and lovely, beautiful democracy rah rah but actually, what can one MP really do? Oh, what cynics you all are. There is actually an encouraging amount a single MP can do, even from the backest of benches. Mark Ballard had never intended to be a politician: he put his name down on the Green party's list for the Scottish parliament just to make up the numbers, and promised his girlfriend that, even with proportional representation, he'd never be elected. And then, in 2003, he was. He was surprised at how much influence he had in his four years as an MSP: "It took me a while, but I felt by the end of my term I was really getting better at doing things. I think that the presence of the Green group in the Scottish parliament meant that questions got asked that would not otherwise have been asked, and policies had to be put in place in order to answer those questions."

MPs can help you to lobby the actual government, to begin with; this is different from lobbying the MPs, and harder. Moy points out: "The best time to lobby is before decisions are made public, which requires good luck or civil service connections, which aren't easy to get. Individuals generally can't lobby the government directly, unlike large organisations. One thing an MP might be able to arrange for a campaigner is a meeting with officials. They shouldn't imagine this is a snub: those are the people who will advise the minister what a policy should be. If you come across as serious, constructive and well informed, you can get a long way with officials."

MPs can also put down early day motions (known in the Welsh Assembly as statements of opinion and in Northern Ireland as no named day motions). These are essentially in-house petitions that other MPs sign up to. Very few of these are even debated, but they're useful for knowing who's interested in your topic, and if they attract enough signatures they do get noticed.

Your pet MP can set up an APG or a cross-party group if there isn't one already in existence – as in the case of carbon rationing. You can even offer to help him run it: nearly half of all APGs receive administrative assistance from lobbyists or charities or trade organisations. (Some also receive financial assistance, which sounds excitingly tawdry but turns out to be things such as the climate change APG's "£1,072 from the Environment Council in relation to costs incurred in holding a parliamentary reception". Right or wrong? Hmm. We will move on from that.)

He can also send questions to the relevant department, and ask questions in the Commons. Again, these won't necessarily elicit lightning action, but they will put up little signs in the heads of other MPs that this subject needs to be thought about.

And if your MP thinks he's getting enough interest, he can start to consider putting in a private member's bill (PMB). This basically means a bill that is not put forward by the government but that doesn't mean the government won't back it if there seems to be enough support in the country. PMBs get through on a fairly regular basis – in the 2005–06 session for example, of the 56 bills that received royal assent three were PMBs, while in the revolutionary 1996–7 session no fewer than 22 got through. They were on subjects such as "confiscation of alcohol (young persons)", "pharmacists (fitness to practise)" and "police (health and safety)". PMBs since have covered "warm homes and energy conservation", "pesticides" and "gang-masters" – perhaps the very subjects on which you are campaigning.

Ron Bailey, I was told, is the country's foremost expert on private members' bills. When I met him, he had just pulled off what he called the biggest job of his life. "When I started this," he says, "I knew it was on the edge of what's conceivable." He's a lifelong activist, who started campaigning on conditions in hostels for the homeless in the 60s, then helped to kick off the squatting movement of the 70s, before transferring his considerable energies to the House of Commons. He has helped to get at least five bills through (including the warm homes bill mentioned above) but is rubbing his hands with glee over the latest, the sustainable communities bill, which he thinks has the potential to turn government upside down. A little bit anyway. (He tells me very firmly that he's not a lobbyist, by the way. All right?)

"The main part of my work, at least four-fifths of it, isn't actually in the House of Commons – it's out there in the country, running round and round getting support going for the bills. You don't even start on the bill until you know you've got a proper amount of support for it, and you do that by going to meetings, getting in touch with people – I collect databases of names – just creating momentum and support for it, and getting them to write to their MPs and getting it all moving. Then, and only then, do you start talking to MPs." He was funded by a group of businessmen who put money behind green projects: he explained to them that this could be a tough bill and they were pretty into it. The sustainable communities bill basically requires the government to publish action plans for making local communities sustainable, and for stopping decline; in order to publish these action plans (this is the bit Bailey is so excited about) the government is compelled by law to consult local councils, and the local councils are compelled to set up citizens' panel and reach agreement with them (not just consult, but agree) on what needs to be done. So get yourself on a citizens' panel now: you will have direct control over what happens to your area! Anyway. This is why Bailey thought it was going to be such a hard sell.

"But the point of building all that support out in the country," he says, "is so that when you finally introduce the bill – which Nick Hurd MP was kind enough to do – MPs already know about it. I was in the Commons tea room one day, and overheard some

MPs talking about it: one of them mentioned it and another said, 'Oh yes, I got a couple of letters about that,' and then another one said, yes, he had too. And that's it – you're off. After that you have to keep it safe through the House, make sure that no one is going to change the wording. I had to keep explaining to people that they couldn't have a "consultation"; they needed to have a duty to cooperate. We had a huge battle with the civil service." The bill received royal assent on October 23 2007. Bailey was already thinking about his next project.

It's also worth watching what parliamentary committees are up to, and trying to get in to present evidence to them. If, for example, you want some input into the latest amendment to the freedom of information bill, or you hear that the health committee is launching an enquiry into health inequalities, you might consider submitting written evidence. The committee will usually have set up an email address, so you need to put together a document, no longer than 3,000 words, with numbered paragraphs, an executive summary, your name, contact details (address and telephone number), and a bit of biography. It might even be worth contacting the committee to see if you can give oral evidence. If you've already been in contact with members of the committee on behalf of your campaign group, or if your pet MP is involved, this will of course give you a head start. The big lobby groups will be in there already, making love to everyone who might give them a hand, but there's no reason you can't be hustling for your cause too.

Finally, you can ask parliamentary representatives to table amendments to government bills: these don't sound like much but can turn out to be significant. This is what Trickett did with the 2006 Companies Act, which was one of the biggest pieces of legislation ever to go through the House of Commons. It was mostly about deregulation, and almost entirely favourable to British business: there had originally been a plan to compel businesses to produce operating and financial reviews that might have made them more accountable, but that was unexpectedly dropped by Gordon Brown.

At the last minute Trickett came forward with a clause obliging directors of public companies to include in their annual review anything that might harm profits because it endangers the company's reputation. So a company that is in danger of failing to comply with carbon reduction targets would ideally report this instead of burying it before the greenwash-watchers get hold of it, while another company facing a union dispute in a developing country should also raise the matter in its report. It's hard to know how seriously companies will take the requirement, however, or who will challenge them if they fail to comply.

Trickett is an engaging man, who leans back in his seat and sticks his feet on the desk while talking – briefly to me and then to some campaigners who he is trying to goad into stirring up more trouble. "We have to wait now: in a few months time companies will be starting to put in their annual general reports, and they will have to take this amendment into account. And then we'll be able to see what we can do with this. In the meantime, what else can we get up to?" The amendment is not exactly a gun to corporate heads, but it has interesting possibilities, and all Trickett needed to do was table it before the Speaker, with the signatures of 50 likeminded MPs to indicate that he had support. And, of course, persuade the government to let it through, which is where quick wits and a good heft of external pressure come in handy.

They're all there, waiting for your call, so off you go. Congratulations, by the way: you are now a lobbyist. Have you told your mother?

Chapter Nine
The unions

In the middle of summer – the terrible rainy summer of 2007, where even to look at a tent peg brought black clouds scudding over the horizon – a couple of friends and I loaded sleeping bags into the back of a Mini and set off for the Dorset village of Tolpuddle. "Will there be quality men there?" one of my friends wanted to know. "Oh yes," I promised. "The Tolpuddle martyrs' festival is famous for being stacked with good-looking single men. Trade union activists don't have time to find girlfriends, and they're always very thin and handsome and intense and sex-mad from all that plotting to overthrow the state. They'll fall upon you like tigers." Of course it was not entirely true. The crowd at Tolpuddle is a lovely one, but sex-mad is probably not the first adjective that springs to mind.

They're more likely to turn up with folding chairs (for when Tony Benn makes his speech) than packets of condoms, more prone to talk about real ale than the mysterious power of your gaze. On Saturday night the comedian Mark Thomas did a set, followed by the band Baghdaddies; we downed a fair amount of alcohol and had a good boogie. At midnight the festival shut down, just as the rain began, and we trudged back to the tent seeing lights going out one by one around us. "Where's the after-show party?" moaned my friend. "Where's the rock'n'roll?"

The rain fell gently upon our tent all night, and was still falling the next morning as I poked my head out of the opening to look down a grey, drenched festival field. We walked back down the main tent and found that the Women's Institute had arrived, just like the cavalry. They had lined up little one-ring stoves in a row along trestle tables and were cooking a fry-up, item by item. So you moved along the table, and out of the first pan came mushrooms, and out of the second came bacon, and so on until you reached the end where a bearded gentleman (the vicar, I think) had five toasters lined up in front of him and was running up and down them like a xylophone player, trying to find toast that was, well, toasted. Shortly after that the tent was cleared so that the socialist book fair could set up for the rest of the day, with a break for the local school to perform their interpretation of the Tolpuddle martyrs' tale. The rain continued. And my friends went back to sleep and were not seen again by anyone until shortly before it was time to leave.

But I had a fantastic time. I'd arranged to meet the singer Billy Bragg (who performs there every year) for a chat at one o'clock, but before that I had to go on the annual march through the tiny village. I was coming past the churchyard just as they laid the wreaths on the graves of the Tolpuddle martyrs. The Bristol Socialist Choir, all in tight red T-shirts with the name of their organisation in yellow across their magnificent chests, sang the Internationale, and everyone wiped their eyes, and when I explained to Bragg why I was late he nodded. "You've gotta make time for the Bristol Socialist Choir," he said wisely. "If there was ever a good reason for being late, that's it."

In case you don't know the story of the Tolpuddle martyrs (everyone should but I admit I was a bit fuzzy on the details, too), they were a group of agricultural workers who, in 1834, decided to form a "friendly society" (a kind of proto-union) to protest against the fall in wages. The Combination Acts that had been passed to stamp out this sort of thing during the 1790s were relaxed in 1824. But at the same time the whole workforce of Britain was being industrialised at a clattering pace, and parliament was failing to keep up and provide any kind of new protection. As the industrialists exploited their work-force to the utmost, the need for a bit of solidarity among workers was more and more urgent.

The local magistrate, James Frampton (may his name be cursed forever!), was furious when he heard about the society and managed to dredge up a 1797 law against oath-taking; six of the labourers were chucked into prison, tried and transported. But where a few years earlier this might have been the end of the story, now there was uproar. The trial had obviously been rigged – one of the labourers, George Loveless, wrote an account that showed the judge putting words into the mouths of the prisoners and blatantly directing the jury – and a similar case elsewhere in England had been dismissed. The furore reached such a pitch that the "martyrs" were granted a free pardon and allowed to come back to Britain. Loveless, already in Australia, heard of the pardon shortly after sending for his wife and children, and faced an agonising dilemma over whether to wait for them and then try to find the money to take everyone back home, or to travel back at once and leave his nearest and dearest stranded down under. The authorities had offered him free passage back home – but only if he set off immediately. At the last minute a letter arrived from his wife saying she was still at home, and he boarded the ship for London.

So they weren't martyrs in quite the way you'd expect, in that most of them died in comfort at home in their own village. But their victory drew a line for all "combinations" of workers after them: the establishment would never dare to treat organisers in quite this way again. The working classes had at last found their voice.

Tony Benn, clearly deeply loved by the Tolpuddle crowd, who nod and smile in a maternal way as he wanders about and shakes hands and signs autographs, always delivers the keynote speech. This time he told the crowd that after the doctor had fitted his new pacemaker, he'd told him to give Tolpuddle a miss for once. "But I must come to Tolpuddle!" he said. "It is my heart! Tolpuddle is what keeps me going!" Cheers and tears all round. But it was impossible not to worry, as we wallowed joyfully in nostalgia, that perhaps the trade union movement was showing its age. Membership peaked in 1979 and has been declining steadily ever since, presently standing at just over half the number of those long-gone days. The average union member earns 12.5 per cent more than their non-union colleagues, but Margaret Thatcher's "reforms" have made it much harder to call and win strikes, and today's casualised, globalised workforce is immensely hard to mobilise. There is not the automatic support for strikers that there once was, even amongst their traditional constituencies.

And yet, I like to imagine the union movement as Wile E Coyote, battered and exploded, yet pulling itself together for one more attack. Recent years have been about reassessment, and finding a new way, but many union members believe that they have begun to do that, by being much more proactive in recruiting new members, forming coalitions with single-issue campaign groups on subjects such as sweat-shop workers and casual workers, relaxing the idea of the trade-based unions and making them far more inclusive, and adopting a new kind of internationalism that's not just about voting in a motion of solidarity but actually applying pressure in several places at once. Membership is still heading downwards in a lot of unions, but else-where it has stabilised and in some cases is even rising again.

It seems to be all about trying to break the old stereotypes: the closed-shop, I'm All Right Jack caricature of the 1970s striker is slowly eroding, although it's a long process. What emerges must be able to attract women (who are now joining faster than men) and white-collar workers, and deal with a faster-moving and more flexible working world. At the same time it cannot afford to alienate the people who have always been the heart of the union movement. Tricky …

What can a union do for you? Well, in general terms, it will work to protect your rights within your workplace, represent your inter-ests in the wider world, and fight on your behalf to improve conditions for workers in casualised and low-paid industries (solidarity is not a particularly trendy idea at the moment, but I'm sure it's on its way back in). If you are organising a march, make sure you get the unions involved – they are better than anyone in the world at getting people out, if they think it's in their interests. You will be surprised quite how wide those interests are.

Three stories to give you a flavour of the modern union. The first is only unfurling now, but could be significant: in 2007 an early day motion in the House of Commons asked that trade union environmental representatives be given the same rights at work as other union reps. The idea was that it would be their job specifically to deal with environmental policies in the office such as recycling, turning the heating down, and whatever else their imagination comes up with. This, it must be said, would be an incredibly useful thing. You do really need to have one person in charge of these things – like the chalk monitor at school: just find the person who'll take it incredibly seriously and get a bit obsessive about it and then cheer them on, and then win Green Office of the Year and all drink a lot of cava … which can't be bad. If the unions begin to extend their remit into environmental responsibility, it will be a huge step forward for greenies.

The second has been going for a while, and has really caused fireworks in the US. The Living Wage campaign started life in Baltimore in 1994 when people working in homeless shelters and soup kitchens noticed that their visitors increasingly had full-time jobs. The federal minimum at that time was $4.25 an hour (approximately £2.80 at 1994 exchange rates); a campaign group got together and managed to persuade the city council to raise the basic pay for city contract workers to $6.10. After that it occurred to campaigners that perhaps city councils in other parts of the country might be able to raise minimum wages in general: the Living Wage campaign has spread since then all over the country, most famously to the wealthy city of Santa Fe. Carol Oppenheimer, a labour attorney, described the campaign's masterstroke to the American journalist Jon Gertner: "What really got the other side was when we said, 'It's just immoral to pay people $5.15 – they can't live on that.' It made the businesspeople furious. And we realised then that we had something there, so we said it over and over again. Forget the economic argument; this was a moral one. It made them crazy. And we knew that was our issue." In 2003 Santa Fe's minimum wage became the country's highest – $8.50.

The result has been a fierce argument throughout the US about the impact on local employment and small businesses (although the Santa Fe ordinance exempts anyone who employs fewer than 25 people). It hasn't slowed the campaign for "a living wage", however, which, by 2009 had more than 75 groups running in towns and cities across the States. And it has spread to other countries. In the UK, for example, a campaign group called London Citizens has joined up with the Transport and General Workers' Union to get corporations to make a commitment that their cleaners and other agency workers are paid a living wage: HSBC, Morgan Grenfell, Lehmann Brothers, Royal Bank of Scotland and Deutsche Bank are among those to have signed up. So unions are learning to deal with the new problems arising in this casualised world, and starting to form links with the agency workers who previously would have been regarded as deadly foes.

Why I fight

Billy Bragg

Singersongwriter; one of the founders of the musicians' collective Red Wedge, which campaigned for Labour in the 80s

It's very difficult to measure how something as intangible and ephemeral as song can change the world. I've thought about it a lot and I've been asked about it a lot – it's the old challenge that they always throw down at you. All I can throw back is my own experience and how my world was changed by music, at the Rock Against Racism concert in 1978. Up to that point I hadn't been overly political – in fact, Rock Against Racism was the first political thing I ever did. I was aware of the National Front, I didn't like the National Front, but I was working in a place where there was a lot of casual racism, a lot of sexism and homophobia, and I never said anything. I was only a kid, really, and I just went along with it.

And then I went on this Rock Against Racism march because the Clash, who were one of my favourite bands, were involved. It was extraordinary to go into the park in Hackney and see 100,000 people just like me, and it convinced me that this is what my generation was going to do. This was how we were going to be different from the previous generation. We weren't going to make our stand on peace and long hair – that wasn't the front line any more. The front line was racism and opposing fascism. When I went back to work on Monday morning I was confident enough to start standing up to the casual racism and sexism and homophobia.

Our job as musicians is to draw people together. That's the role that music plays: it creates an audience. And you can do a number of things with that audience – you can sell 'em records, but you can also give them a powerful message and send them away with a different perspective. You have the opportunity to do that. You know how music can lift you up – it's just whether you can do anything positive with that, other than just get off on it. Speaking as a punter, I know that through listening to the music of the Clash my perspective of the world was changed for ever in a way that still inspires me.

Thirdly, and finally, the old unions are transforming themselves. The old steel workers' union ISTC, for one, now known as Community, is energetically scooping up new members. It now represents a much wider constituency, including betting-shop employees. One of its most famous recruitment drives involved handing out condoms to the staff of a non-union Scottish computer hardware firm, with the slogan "There's more than one form of protection – join a union!" Thanks to this and other less sensational approaches, union membership at one point reached 75 per cent.

If you are not a member of a union, and you believe there is no union that serves you, think again. Perhaps you could get in touch with the Trades Union Congress, the overarching body, in order to find out what exists? It's important: you are upholding a right that has been hard-won. Even if you don't need the unions this week, you may need them the next. And in the meantime they are campaigning on behalf of sweatshop workers, casual workers, all the little people who need support. You need someone at your back.

The law and ... union membership, strikes and pickets

You have the right to be a member of a union, state the Universal Declaration of Human Rights and the European Convention on Human Rights. Any employer who tries to pressure you or even threatens you with the sack over union activities is acting illegally.

In Britain you do not, however, have a positive right to strike: it is not quite as straightforward as that. Instead the law protects trade unions and their employees from liability in relation to an action: so, for example, a union can't be sued for inducing its members to break their employment contract by taking industrial action, and an employee may be able to put in a claim for unfair dismissal if he is sacked for carrying out industrial action.

But these immunities apply only if you are carrying out a protected action – ie, if the union is backing you, has held a secret ballot to make sure there is majority backing for your strike, and has complied with other procedural requirements (such as serving notices of the ballot result and industrial action plans on the employees). If the union hasn't held a ballot, then strikers can legally all be fired (though for some odd reason they all have to be fired at once in this situation, which is a fairly massive gamble).

And if you just walk out on unofficial strike action and the union doesn't back you, then strikers can be fired one by one, or however the boss wants to do it.

Once you are on strike, it is, of course, the moment to get picketing. By law a picket is required to be peaceful (no threatening or abusive language, no obstruction of the highway or entrance to the workplace, no intimidation); at or close to the employee's workplace; and connected to a trade dispute involving the picketing employee.

If this is not the case, the employer is entitled to get an injunction preventing the picketing.

What about solidarity action? Well, you the striker are allowed to try to talk other workers into refusing to honour contracts with your employer. For instance, if you are on strike, you can try to persuade delivery men not to transport goods to your employer. But secondary action – where those same delivery men then go on strike or picket their own place of work in sympathy, or where the original strikers go and picket the contractor – is illegal.

Clearly this situation is far from perfect. The failure to simply provide the right to strike means that the UK has been found to be in breach of ILO conventions on fundamental trade union rights by the ILO Committee of Experts; as well as in breach of the European Social Charter of 1961 by the European Committee on Social Rights, and of article 11 of the European Convention on Human Rights in the landmark ASLEF case. In France, Greece, Italy, Portugal, Spain and Sweden, the right to strike is explicitly recognised. This is what unions in the UK have been agitating for here, especially in discussions of a potential British Bill of Rights.

A further problem is that the law in its current form does not reflect the way big corporations now subcontract so much of their business. When 1,000 BA workers walked out at Heathrow in August 2005 in sympathy with striking workers at Gate Gourmet, one of BA's contractors, their action was officially secondary action unprotected by any legal immunities. But as far as they were concerned, they were all part of the same organisation. Unions want to see modernisation here too.

Chapter Ten
Getting the facts

Establishing the facts must be one of the most important planks of any campaign. In the simplest possible terms, information is power. And besides, the whole thing will go straight down the toilet if, when Jeremy Paxman turns to you and asks (his lip curling sexily upwards) "How can you prove this?", you cough, splutter, and mutter something about getting back to him. Getting the facts for yourself, seeing the realities with your own eyes, is one of the most effective weapons in any campaign's armoury. It's all very well to have passion and conviction, but it's even better to be right.

Sally Bunday is not a scientist, but 30 years ago when her son Miles was born, she realised that there was something wrong.

"He was a very unsettled baby – he cried a lot and he was always, always restless," she recalls. Finally, when Miles was two and a half, a doctor diagnosed him as extremely hyperactive. "But even then they just offered us some medication and said, 'Send him to nursery.' Then we came across some work by Dr Benjamin Feingold on the link between certain foods and food additives and hyperactivity; we cut out orange squash and chocolate and sweets and within a few weeks he was so much calmer. He still had a hyper side to him, but now he would sit at a table for a whole meal, and bath time wasn't such a struggle."

Other mothers might have left it there, but then Bunday wrote a piece for a women's magazine and thousands of readers wrote to her. She decided she had to look more closely at this.

There was little scientific evidence at the time to back up her theory about the link between food additives and hyperactivity, but over the years she compiled mountains of data from the parents she spoke to. "One young girl," she says, "had a 16-month-old baby who just wouldn't stop crying. I talked through the child's diet with her and she was giving the little girl sugar-free orange squash. As soon as she stopped, her daughter improved beyond recognition." She has since founded the Hyperactive Children's Support Group, built up a compelling case, inundated the Food Standards Agency (and its predecessor MAFF) with letters – "I don't think they like me very much" – and put unrelenting pressure on every other government department that might have something to do with the subject. And slowly her campaign, and that of those who have come to stand beside her, is being vindicated.

Very sadly, several years ago her son was killed in a motorcycle accident. Bunday has not stopped campaigning. MAFF finally commissioned some research in 1999, but then buried the results – which revealed that additives were problematic – until another food campaigner accidentally came across them. The FSA then commissioned another study, which came up with the same results. "But what makes me mad," says Bunday, "is that they're too cowardly, even now, to do anything about it. Why can't they just take action? We're eating more and more processed food and our children are getting more aggressive, more obese, more disruptive; can no one see the connection? I'm even more frustrated now then I was, but I keep plodding on." It is inevitable, however, that at some point soon the FSA will be forced to take action on food additives. The measures will probably fall well short of what campaigners want – they always do – but the thing will be started.

The slave trade abolitionists, at the end of the 18th century, helped to pioneer the idea of using investigation as part of a campaign: Thomas Clarkson and James Stephens between them spent many hours gathering testimony about slave ship experiences and eventually presented 850 pages to parliament. In their wake came the likes of Robert Bald, who reported on conditions in the Scottish mines and desperately campaigned against women's employment there, and Flora Tristan, who visited the brothels of London and found children as young as 10, as she wrote in her London Journal. But the reporting of injustice and iniquity really came of age in the 1830s and 40s as the English and the Scots moved in their hundreds of thousands into the cities, where they worked 15-hour days in factories. The squalid world in which they found themselves shocked and infuriated observers such as Alexis de Tocqueville, Charles Dickens and Friedrich Engels, Karl Marx's best mate and lifelong colleague.

Engels was the son of a wealthy German mill-owner (who ended up indirectly funding Marx for many years – always quite an enjoyable thought). In 1842 his father sent him to Manchester to work in the company's offices there. Engels managed to hold down the day job, which let him send money regularly to Marx, but spent his free time in the slums with his lover, Mary Burns.

Two years later he produced The Condition of the Working Classes in England in 1844, a scrupulous document that describes, street by street, town by town, factory by factory, the way in which the vast majority of England's citizens were living. Of Manchester, to which he devoted most space, he writes: "The town itself is peculiarly built, so that a person may live in it for years, and go in and out daily without coming into contact with a working-people's quarter or even with workers ... I know very well that this hypocritical plan is more or less common to all great cities ... but at the same time, I have never seen so systematic a shutting out of the working class from the thoroughfares, so tender a concealment of everything which might affront the eye and the nerves of the bourgeoisie, as in Manchester."

Engels, however, did go into the slum areas, a collection of court-yards reached along covered passages from the main street. "He who turns in thither gets into a filth and disgusting grime, the equal of which is not to be found ... In one of these courts there stands directly at the entrance, at the end of the covered passage, a privy without a door, so dirty that the inhabitants can pass into and out of the court only by passing through foul pools of stagnant urine and excrement ... "

Along Ducie Bridge, he reported, "the condition of the dwellings on both banks grown worse rather than better. He who turns to the left here from the main street, Long Millgate, is lost: he wanders from one court to another, turns countless corners, passes nothing but narrow filthy nooks and alleys, until after a few minutes he has lost all clue and knows not whither to turn. Everywhere half or wholly ruined buildings, some of them actually uninhabited, which means a great deal here; rarely a wooden or stone floor to be seen in the houses, almost uniformly broken, ill-fitting windows and doors, and a state of filth! Everywhere heaps of debris, refuse and offal; standing pools for gutters and a stench which alone would make it impossible for any human being in any degree civilised to live in such a district ... Such is the Old Town of Manchester."

Within three years the government, responding to widespread unrest and demand for change – not least from the reformers known as the Chartists, with whom Engels and Marx were both involved – had limited factory hours for women and young people to 10 hours a day. In 1848 the first Public Health Act allowed local boards of health to be set up, although it would take another 30 years for the government to get really serious about drainage and sanitation.

Newspaper editors began to realise that poking and prodding around could be useful to them, both to expose evil and to sell papers. When cholera broke out in 1849 the journalist Henry Mayhew (who had earlier founded Punch magazine but was now broke) persuaded his editor John Black at the Morning Chronicle to let him look into it. Black agreed and put a team on to it – the first time any newspaper had done such a thing. Mayhew's revelatory articles – attacked by the Economist as "unthinkingly increasing the enormous funds already profusely destined to charitable purposes" and "encouraging a reliance on public sympathy for help instead on self-exertion" – were later published as the collections London Labour and The London Poor. I speak as a journalist when

I say that we are in general a bunch of freeloaders – but we have our uses too. Good investigative journalists have the same instincts as good campaigners – a sprinkling of doubt about the status quo coupled with a desire to poke about a bit, to stick their noses where it's not wanted, to reach conclusions that probably won't suit those in power. Other great exposés include Annie Besant's probing of the working conditions of the match girls in the 1880s, Woodward and Bernstein's unstoppable exposure of Nixon during Watergate, Robert Parry's examination of the Iran–Contra operation in Reagan's White House in the 80s and, most recently, Seymour Hersh's dissection of the Bush administration's conduct during the invasion and occupation of Iraq. There's a whole genre of investigative journalism now, and although some of it exists just to fill newspaper columns, or lend a veneer of respectability to down-market TV stations, one hopes that it can act as a kind of watchdog on industry and government. At best, a decision may occasionally be taken not to cut corners because otherwise "that bloody annoying git Donal Macintyre might come round".

It is, of course, one thing to talk about doing a bit of investigation and quite another to do it. But, although Roger Cook will not thank me for saying this, anyone can investigate something. The most useful qualities are patience and determination and the ability to put things together in your head. Most of the time the facts are readily available, and if they're not you may learn something just by asking why. You need a phone, a library ticket, an internet connection and you're off.

The modern world is full of specialists, and they all want us to think you need a postgraduate degree to understand law, or planning, or parliamentary procedure, or corporation strategies, but actually that's rubbish. Most of the time the facts are readily available, and if they're not you may learn something just by asking why. Whatever you're fighting, the building of a local supermarket, say, make sure you get all the information you can ...

Look at the McLibel case, where two campaigners battled one

of the world's biggest corporations in the English courts. Helen Steel and Dave Morris, who spent seven years defending themselves against charges of libelling the fast-food giant, did have some legal advice from people such as Keir Starmer, who is now one of the country's premier human rights lawyers, but it was they who were in court day after day, and it was they who managed to get at least one of McDonalds' own witnesses to double back and contradict themselves in a way that would make the grandest of barristers proud. (They then went on to the European courts, but that's another story.)

Why I fight

Julie White
Environmental campaigner

I started campaigning on roads while I was still doing my medical degree; I went along to the Newbury bypass campaign and was also involved in the campaign to stop the expansion of Manchester airport. I think if you're a doctor, you're concerned with people's health, and from that it's a natural step to be concerned with climate change, which is, I really believe, the biggest problem facing us by far. Some specialists or hospital doctors might focus quite narrowly on treatment, but if you're in public health, or a GP like me, you're inevitably concerned with a patient's environment.

Tinsley, the area of Sheffield where I practise, is completely overshadowed by the M1, which goes on legs right through it. It's a poor area anyway, because it's always poorer people who are forced to live in areas by big roads, but the rate of hospital admission for asthma in Tinsley is double that of the whole of the rest of Sheffield. It's noisy here too – in the schools the teachers have to shut their windows in order to be heard in the classrooms – and the pollution seems to make everything dirtier faster.

There's more and more research going on into the effects of pollution on our health. It's like smoking and lung cancer – it takes a long time to prove a direct causal relation, but the more research that's done, the more it becomes impossible to deny. I'm pretty sure this is going to take over my life for the next couple of years.

Doggedness and discipline, then, must be your watchwords, whether you're investigating a clothing manufacturer's use of child labour or challenging a planning application. If you're fighting the building of a supermarket, for example, make sure you get all the information you can, starting with the planning application, the council's assessment, and the council's local development plan (or whatever title they've given it). Read the paperwork you get. Make notes. Try to work out what you need to know. If you don't understand something, ring up and ask for clarification. Don't worry about sounding stupid, and don't worry if you get someone snotty on the other end of the line. No one knows anything (this is the first law of investigation). Just carry on asking questions until you really understand the situation: that is the point of the exercise. If officials won't help you, try someone such as Planning Aid, a government-funded body that offers free advice.

Be polite to everyone, even if they're being a pain. You never know when you'll need to talk to them again. Try to end the conversation on a friendly note, perhaps mentioning that you might need to phone back for more information. More questions will inevitably crop up as soon as you hang up. Keep neat and legible notes of all your conversations and all your reading. Set up a phone book and note down all the numbers you use, all the people you talk to – this is invaluable. You can make notes about them if you want, to jog your memory if you need to talk to them again in six months, time. It's amazing how easily you forget something (and remembering someone's name when you ring back also has a useful unlocking effect). Write it all down.

Once you've got the first load of information under your belt, what next? More research. You need to be wary of any information you come across, check the sources, pick holes and trust your instinct, because it's worryingly easy to make omissions that distort the truth. For example, you would imagine that an organisation with a name such as the British Nutrition Foundation would be keen to warn the public about the dangers of a diet which includes large quantities of refined carbohydrate. Odd then that their factsheet about sugar makes the stuff sound like your fifth veg helping of the day, coming as it does from beet, "a root crop resembling a large parsnip", and cane, "a very tall grass". A list follows of the different forms of refined sugar and then in one paragraph at the end, we are told that "the main public health issue associated with total sugar consumption is dental health, particularly among those who do not regularly use fluoridated toothpaste." So if you were worried that sugar consumption is connected in any way with life-threatening conditions such as obesity or diabetes, you can relax, there's not a word about either of them. It is no doubt entirely coincidental that among the BNF's paying members are some of the largest food giants in the world.

Even if you want to, you won't be able to match your opponents' budgets and glossy marketing material: the biggest companies can, if they wish, pay for research that will bring in exactly the results they want. But it's possible to pick holes with a bit of energy and imagination.

So, returning to our planning application, look at whether the environmental assessment is flawed, for example. Has the supermarket chain underestimated the amount of extra traffic that will be generated, or the impact on local shops? At this point you need to either phone some experts, or walk round the area yourself.

This is how it can work: when Paul D'Ambra heard that Tesco

was planning to build a supermarket in Trafford, his area of Manchester (a very different Manchester from Engel's hellhole) a couple of years ago, he looked for evidence of how it might affect the local shops, but couldn't find anything. A supermarket chain had already been given permission to build in the nearby town of Burnage, however, so he went there and asked shopkeepers a couple of questions about the plan. "There were 60 shops down there," he recalls, "and at that point they had mixed feelings – some had leaflets in the shops campaigning to keep the supermarket away, but some of them were in favour, thought it would bring more business their way. Within three months of the supermarket opening, however, they were all against it. And after a year three of the shops had closed. There were side effects that none of them had expected, like there was one guy running a computer training company who closed down because he just hadn't realised how much of his trade came from people walking past. The shop doing electrical repairs shut down too – people just went to Tesco and bought a new toaster."

D'Ambra was doing volunteer work for Friends of the Earth at the time. Since he gave FoE this information, it has been used in other planning cases, and is now commonly referred to as the Burnage Survey. D'Ambra also helped to set up a local group to oppose the new Tesco. Luckily for them, they happened to include a planning consultant, which obviously made life easier. But they also carried on with D'Ambra's strategy of getting out in the area: they did a traffic count, for example, which proved that Tesco's planning application had underestimated the congestion that a new store would cause. They dismantled Tesco's assessment of the need for a new supermarket simply by listing the small retailers already present. The town council eventually refused the application.

To summarise: many questions, repeated over and over again.

The law and ... your right to information

Things we would not have known without the Freedom of Information Act 2000:

1. Tony Blair spent £2,000 on cosmetics over six years.
2. The richest landowners get the biggest EU farm subsidies.
3. Margaret Thatcher's government considered sending a team of dolphins to search for the Loch Ness monster.

These are the kind of facts that brighten up the day. Even if New Labour's promises of complete transparency didn't quite work out, we clearly have more access to government information then we did a decade ago.

But how precisely do we get it? In England and Wales there are two principal routes: the freedom of information request, governed by the Freedom of Information (FoI) Act, and the environmental information request, covered by the Environment Information Regulations. The first is for all kinds of recorded information, although the list of exemptions is extremely long; the second, according to the Department for the Environment, relates to:

a) the state of the elements of the environment, such as air and atmosphere, water, soil, land, landscape and natural sites including wetlands, coastal and marine areas, biological diversity and its components; genetically modified organisms, and the interaction among these elements;

b) substances, energy, noise, radiation or waste, including radioactive waste, emissions, discharges and other releases into the environment, affecting or likely to affect the elements of the environment referred to in (a);

c) measures (including administrative measures), such as policies, legislation, plans, programmes, environmental agreements, and activities affecting or likely to affect the environment;

d) reports on the implementation of environmental legislation;

e) cost-benefit and other economic analyses and assumptions used within the framework of the measures and activities referred to in (c); and

f) the state of human health and safety, including the contamination of the food chain, where relevant, conditions of human life, cultural sites and built structures inasmuch as they are or may be affected by the state of the elements of the environment referred to in (a) or, through those elements, by any of the matters referred to in (b) and (c).

Oof. The FoI act entitles you to ask a public authority (which obviously includes the government and local authorities, but also the NHS, the police, and various bodies such as the Tate gallery) what information they have on a subject, and then to have that information communicated to you. There's no form to fill in: you just need to put your request in writing and send it to the official or organisation you think most likely to be able to help. They must reply within 20 working days. It's genius.

The EIR entitle you to ask "all public authorities" for information related to the environment. You don't have to do it in writing; a phone call is entirely acceptable. And interestingly, under the EIR private firms – if they are considered to be providing a public service – may also be obliged to follow the regulations. Organisations that the information commissioner has decided fall within the remit of the EIRs have included Network Rail and the Port of London Authority.

Which brings us on to the response to which you are entitled. In both cases, the body in question may just hand the info over, ask for more details from you to clarify the request, or refuse. It can only say no if the material is exempt; unfortunately, the list of exemptions is as long as your arm. Under the FoI act, information can be withheld if the request is vexatious; if it would cost a lot of money to comply; if the information is readily available elsewhere; if the information is going to be published anyway within a reasonable timeframe; if its disclosure is likely to prejudice international relations; if its disclosure would prejudice relations between two administrations in the UK; if it would prejudice economic interests of the UK; if it would prejudice law enforcement interests or if the information is being held specifically in relation to an investigation or other criminal proceeding; if it would prejudice the government's conduct of public affairs ... In other words, if they really don't want you to see it, they can come up with something.

If you feel a decision was unfair, you can ask the Information Commissioner to look into the case. The public authority must abide by the decision, but if you are unhappy with the commissioner's ruling you have a further right of appeal to the Information Tribunal. The Environment Information Regulations operate similarly.

Scotland has its own parallel EIR and FoI requests; they work in the same way, although the exemptions are not completely identical. But in a way the wording of the exemptions doesn't really matter: as I said, if they want to find a way to stop you having the information, they can.

But campaigners and journalists have managed, very effectively, to use these acts in order to extract all sorts of bits of information. It was a Freedom of Information request, for example, which triggered the recent MPs expenses scandal, and which has had a lasting impact on British politics.

As always, you'll find contact details at the end of this book.

Chapter Eleven
Getting publicity

On Tony Blair's very last day in office a peace activist called Sue managed to get herself a prime position near Downing Street, with a handful of eggs at the ready, all primed to chuck at his car. "But I didn't realise he'd drive off on the other side of the road," she lamented later that evening, when I bumped into her at an anti-war campsite on Parliament Green. "I thought he was so law-abiding, but they went off on the other side and I missed completely. The police asked me for my name and address, and I said, 'I don't think I need to give you those.' And then they said that as I'd just attempted an arrestable offence" – lobbing eggs at the soon-to-be ex-PM – "I would have to give my name and date of birth at least. And then, after one of them had walked off, the other one said to me, 'Nearly got him, though!'

Everyone laughed. It's always a heartening thing for a campaigner to get an unexpected demonstration of solidarity from a complete outsider. Gabriel, another activist, said: "Really, whether or not you hit the car doesn't really matter. The real measure of success in any mission is obviously, 'Did it make anyone laugh?'"

A protest or a campaign does not exist in a vacuum. The way in which it is perceived by society will have a tremendous effect on its success or failure. You need to "communicate your issues", in classic campaignerspeak. Public sympathy is key for some campaigners: if you manage to win it, you are a long way down the road to victory.

Any campaign that chooses to address the public has two aims, the second of which it hopes will unfurl, like a flower, from the first.

The first aim is to put information that it holds into the public domain so that it becomes part of the collective consciousness. The second aim is that out of guilt, or shock, or just collective agreement, this information will be acted on, either by the public or by the authorities.

So basically what you're talking about is the power of knowledge, and the power of shame. All very garden of Eden, really. Why does shame or the possibility of it have such a powerful effect? Mark Thomas, who is a virtuoso when it comes to playing on companies' guilty consciences, says it's pretty straightforward: "Corporations and the individuals in them have to live in the real world, so it doesn't matter if they can rig committees or influence votes or arrange inquiries or mount advertising campaigns – they also have to meet their mates, friends, colleagues and pick their kids up from school. They live in the world, and all of us are concerned about how we are seen and what the world thinks of us. The whole point of shame is that it is public – they can disregard my opinion, but if it helps other people have a negative one of them, then that is where it starts to hurt.

"Corporations have a public image that they spend billions on developing and maintaining. Coca-Cola spend about $2bn a year on advertising, they have Santa Claus in their colours, Christmas is their peak time for sales, so none of this would sit well if they were being accused of using child labour in their sugar mills. You want to celebrate Christmas and kids as part of your sales pitch? Then don't use child labour because it will bite you on the arse and you look like a phoney shitbag obsessed only with money, and that is not the message the company wants to promote. If a brand is recognisable across the world, then the universality of the brand is also a weakness. So shame works because it exposes the company. And bad PR means less money."

(In 2004 Human Rights Watch produced a report on child labour in the sugar mills of El Salvador: Coca-Cola was specifically named in the report because they sourced, at the time, from one of the largest mills in the country. They stated in response that they did not condone child labour, had a strict policy against their direct suppliers using child labour and would investigate any such allegations. Since then they've initiated a programme to reduce child labour in general in El Salvador.)

But how do you get the information out there in the first place? That is what this chapter is all about.

The news media

News is what most campaigners/protestors think of when they want to get their issue over to the public and win that crucial sympathy. But how do you do that? In the early 21st century, news is an enormous sprawling beast, communicated through the radio, TV, newspapers, magazines and the internet. And if you want to raise awareness of an issue, you are going to have to interact with the media. (It's very sad, but there's no way round it. As Chris Rose says in his excellent guide to campaigning: "Once you learn how to gain access, it can be entrancing, flattering and addictive, so be careful." That's us, oh yes.)

First and foremost, don't bother with all this if it's not one of your stated aims. Too many organisations waste time trying to get coverage when it will make no difference to their campaign. But if getting press is part of your masterplan, then be strategic about it. Do you want to get editorial coverage (that means being written or talked about, rather than taking out an ad)? Then work out where you want to get coverage, who you are trying to reach. Your area? Then you need to get to know the local paper, the local news TV and any local radio stations. The opinion-makers? The broadsheets. Middle England? The Mail. The rest of the country? Television or radio. The red-tops, as a rule, are interested in campaigns only if they involve donkeys, angry mums or breasts.

Then take a look at your medium. Where would an item about your campaign fit? Do you want to do an upbeat story or a more serious one? You may be under the delusion that all you need to do is tell a journalist what's bugging you and he or she will immediately leap into action on your behalf. You are wrong. Journalists are usually very busy, and lazy, and inundated with press releases and phone calls; mostly, unless you present them with an actual story they won't bother to look into it. If you send a journalist a press release saying, for example, "Houses to be built on field", there's not a lot that can be done with that. They'll yawn and bin it. But if you make it into a story – "Rare bird species threatened by housing development" – perhaps then the journalist's ears will prick up.

What is a story, you ask? The concept is one with which many journalists struggle for ever – but it basically means That Which Is New. The journalist's job is partly to keep an eye on how the world and society are changing, and alert readers to any changes that they may or may not like. So editors want facts that are new to readers, and will perhaps change their perception of the world. But the other aspect of the job is entertainment, and editors are also looking out for whatever tickles them, in the hope that it will tickle their readers too. So get to know the medium in question – watch the programme a few times, or read the paper – and look out for the sort of things it covers, and try to spot the journalists who cover your patch.

You need to get to know your cause really well. If you're trying to stop developers pulling down an old building, for instance, look into its history. Was someone famous married there? Are there some great old photographs of it? If you're campaigning against obesity among children in your area, come up with some amazing facts about them: three out of four teenagers at the local high school sneak out to the chip shop at lunchtime, say. That's a perfect story for a local paper – and it's got a ready-made picture to go with it. You will need to keep coming up with stories like this if you want a high-profile campaign: the better and more interesting the information, the more likely that it will filter through to the national papers as well. If you manage to uncover information about teachers sneaking out to buy chips too, or even running little black-market chip businesses, you could have a story that will end up in the Daily Mail.

Now you want to write a press release; this is governed by strict rules. Ideally it should be no more than one side of A4, with an interesting headline – "Teachers caught red-handed down the chippy" – for example, and then a very lucid first paragraph that says who, what, where, when, and possibly how and why. Something like "Teachers are sneaking out to fast food joints to buy food for pupils, a local obesity campaign group has discovered." If you've got photographs, so much the better. If you've got film, you might even get it on TV. Mention what you have on the press release, and send it out, by email or snail mail, to the journalists who you have identified as probable targets. And there you have it – national media coverage for your issue. It's so easy! (Until the next day when nothing appears and it turns out that the editor has taken against the story and spiked it, and all that effort has been completely wasted.)

Stunts are the route that many campaign groups use these days. Some – such as Fathers 4 Justice, the men campaigning for increased rights for fathers in custody battles – are geniuses at the attention grabbing game. Environmental campaigners use this widely too; getting tonnes of people together to make huge words or numbers, for example, or staging flash picnics at Heathrow airport, or climbing up onto the roofs of the Houses of Parliament. The image gets on the front of the paper, and the group – it hopes – gets a moment to talk about the issue.

There are some modern campaigners who are stunningly good at coming up with stunts (as mentioned above, Fathers 4 Justice is a good example) and who seem to instinctively know how to get their cause all over the papers. I do have one reservation about this tactic, which is that in some ways the amount of press bears no correlation to the worthwhile nature of the cause, but stems, rather, from the talent of the campaigner. But then I suppose that that is always true, no matter what tactic you're looking at.

What about conducting interviews? If a journalist rings you asking questions about your campaign, or wanting you to come on their radio programme or TV show, there are several things to bear in mind. First and foremost, know what you need to say. If a journo catches you unawares, you may not put your case quite as well, so remember you can always claim it's a bad moment and ask them to ring back later, which will give you time to collect your thoughts. Make a list of the things you want to get over – about three points is ideal – and have concrete examples to go with them. For example, if you're talking about the problem of drug use in the park, mention that park-keepers collected five syringes that morning alone. If you're talking about battery hens, compare the life cycle of a battery hen and a free-range hen. Make sure that you are being accurate in what you're saying: whatever you do, don't make something up, because it will come back to haunt you, and discredit you with the journalist and the public.

If you're doing a broadcast interview, make sure you've watched or listened to the programme in question so that you know the format and the approach it takes to guests. Think about your appearance – it may not matter to you, but your message will be better received by the shallow masses out there if you've at least combed your hair and got the egg out of your beard. If you are offered make-up, accept it. Don't wear stripes or eye-bending patterns: the camera doesn't like them. If you can choose between glasses and contacts, choose the contacts, as studio lights reflect off glasses and distract from what you're saying.

What about answering the actual questions? One campaigner suggests playing the scared amateur in order to get the questions in advance; tell them it will help you to prepare and be a bit less nervous. If you manage to wangle this, then carefully plan your answers. Be aware that if you're going on a pre-recorded programme you may be edited, so look out for places where your sentences can be chopped and the meaning changed. And remember that the audience may know nothing about your subject, so make your points clearly. Try to speak at the same rate as you would if you were telling a story to a small child.

Why I fight

Bill Drummond

Musician and founder of No Music Day. In the 90s the KLF became infamous for machine-gunning the audience from at the Brit awards (using blanks, fortunately) and burning £1m

So often people say, "We're going to infiltrate the system and change it from the inside." But it never works. I think what happens nearly every time is that they get changed far faster than the system they're preaching to. It's human nature. You become seduced. And often it's not even the real reason you're doing it: really you want to become part of the system, you want to have the power that the system offers.

I have never identified with the rebel. I've always felt that the classic rebel kicking against the system is actually about being in awe of the system. Really, if they just gave themselves some time instead of kicking and kicking they'd find their own way. When I was doing the KLF, I wanted to try to stay apart from the music industry, but I don't think I was really trying to attack it.

At the time of the Brit awards I was under a lot of stress to do with work, and the way I dealt with it got a little out of control. I was not properly rational, you know? What I'd been planning to do was chop off one of my hands, live on stage, and throw it into the audience. But there was no logic to it – even I could see that – and I got talked out of it. And then I wanted to slaughter a sheep live on stage, but the backing band were all vegetarians and they said, "No way." I didn't see it as a rebellion, you know? I know how my head works, and from time to time it's just like that.

Why did I start No Music Day? Because the technologies that have been evolving have changed our relationship with music. It's become some kind of wallpaper. That offended me, so I wanted to have one day a year where we didn't listen to any music at all. And for some reason it – to make a very bad joke – struck a chord. I didn't go out there and promote this in a big way – it started off as a personal thing – but I set up a website and just got tens of thousands of hits from all over the world. Plus people wanted to do a media story. There's so much sodding media out there, and I suppose this fitted nicely.

Finally, don't hum and haw, or let your eyes wander around the studio too much. Make sure you're looking at the person you're talking to, or the person who is talking. And try to smile occasionally. Even if you're talking about nuclear war, dammit.

But don't forget that there are hundreds of outlets beyond the national papers and television news. The internet has democratised news to some extent – that's the claim, anyway, although of course the same big corporations that own many of the world's newspapers and TV channels are doing their best to buy up the largest and most successful sites. Google now owns the video-sharing website YouTube, while the social networking website MySpace belongs to Rupert Murdoch's News Corporation. But although some internal censorship goes on – such as the removal from YouTube of a video of Tom Cruise addressing his fellow Scientologists – you can still run all sorts of fascinating things. When I searched for "direct action" on YouTube I was flooded with stuff, including films of the Ontario Campaign Against Poverty performing a sit-in, protestors demonstrating against the Iraq war outside the White House in 2007, and Spanish activists defending their squat. The power of using video like this is its directness: there's no substitute for being there, but watching a video is the next best thing. So although it's very hard to target an audience this way, if you can find a way of letting people know that your videos are available, through email perhaps, you may be able to win more support for the next stage of your campaign.

Indymedia is an international chain of autonomous websites that distribute stories that don't make the mainstream press. It's run by activists for activists, and you can't count on it 100 per cent for editorial reliability because the people who run it very clearly have an agenda. However, the same is true of all media to some extent. Indymedia is seen as being for specialists, but that may be precisely who you're aiming at. There are also a number of small independent newsletters and websites, the best known of which is the wonderful Schnews. Its links page is invaluable for getting in touch with other organisations, and finding out more about web-based media.

Index on Censorship: December 2009
"Is Twitter revolutionising revolution?"

In April 2009, I found myself racing up and down Bishopsgate during the G20 protests in London with an aching thumb and deadlines to meet every five minutes or less. I'd been planning to cover the protests in the usual way – notebook, mobile and laptop – but at about 5pm the previous day my editor at the Guardian had announced: "By the way, we'd like you to cover the protests by Twitter tomorrow. Is that okay?"

Tweet I did, all day long, sending 140 character reports back to the Twitter account which the paper had set up for me, trying to remember to include the hashtag (if you put #climatecamp on your tweet it will roll up on your own page and the #climatecamp page, which creates instant open conversations). And I was not the only one. Kate Day from the Daily Telegraph commented that the G20 would "stand out as a turning point for Twitter" and it wasn't the only new tool that came into play with force at the G20. Over the following days, as the policing of the protest came under fire, footage

---

filmed on video phones by protestors and passers-by provided crucial evidence. Even as some newspapers were blaming troublemaking protestors, the footage was giving the lie, revealing to shocked members of the public quite how brutal our boys in blue could be. The circumstances surrounding the death of Ian Tomlinson at the protests (a passer-by who collapsed after being assaulted by a policeman) first emerged when a businessman handed footage from his digital camera to the Guardian. Vital, perhaps revolutionary, new tools had been added to the activist's box.

And that impression was confirmed by the protests in Moldova in Eastern Europe a few days later, which came about, according to Natalia Morar, one of the organisers, "through Twitter, the blogosphere, the internet, SMS, websites. We just met, we brainstormed for 15 minutes, and decided to make a flash mob. In several hours, 15,000 people came out onto the street. None of us could imagine that such a thing could happen, but it shows there exists a very big protest inside society and within young people." And then again, in Iran during the summer of 2009, when thousands of protestors turned out to dispute the results of the presidential elections, leading to running clashes between police and protestors, and estimates of the dead somewhere between 20 (the official figure) and 150. The authorities made attempts to clamp down on internet communication, but Twitter registered streams of tweets, and was used as a news tool by newspapers and networks around the world such as the Guardian, the New York Times and CNN. The US State Department asked Twitter if they would delay downing the site for planned network upgrades, because it would stop Iranians sending out information about the protests. At the same time a brief film of the death of Neda Agha-Soltan, a 27-year-old woman who was shot in the chest while watching the protests, was posted on YouTube and became a rallying point for the opposition (with #neda one of the most frequently used hashtags on Twitter).

Will the new digital technologies revolutionise revolution? Social networking sites are useful for the crucial job of 'getting people out', but once you're on the ground protesting, although it can be informative the technology has its limitations. During the protests in Moldova, there was no mobile network in the square which was the centre of the demonstrations. Nothing, once you're actually there, can beat a megaphone, just as nothing, while you're gearing up for an event, really beats face-to-face meetings.

But what about the second, extremely important, task of getting the message out? For these purposes Twitter and video phones have become astonishingly powerful tools for activists, because they allow people to see events as they unfold and judge for themselves. In the footage of Ian Tomlinson being pushed to the ground by police during the G20 protests, there is a sound, a kind of "whack" at the moment his head hits the pavement (just off the bottom of the screen) which makes the viewer flinch. That one awful moment galvanised an entire country in revulsion (even the notoriously conservative Daily Mail website was filled with horrified comments from readers about police behaviour). The video phone footage of Neda lying on the ground similarly communicates directly with the viewer, it is shocking and unbearably poignant.

Are these technologies helping to deliver the results that the protestors wanted? Surely that is the final test? In the case of Moldova, a few months after the protests the communist government was strategically outflanked by the other political parties and forced to dissolve parliament. However, in the case of the G20 protests my tweeting (11 hours of sending texts from my mobile – my right arm was on fire by the end of the day) along with everyone else's tweeting, turned out to be irrelevant to the story of Ian Tomlinson, which took over the entire narrative of the protests. The wheels of justice continue to grind, but they are grinding the issue of police conduct, rather than the larger issues of climate change and capitalism which the protestors had wanted to highlight. And in Iran, Mahmoud Ahmadinejad's government remains in power, even though sporadic protests break the apparently smooth surface of the regime every couple of months. It will take more than a few tweets to dislodge the authorities there. A few million tweets, however, and the activists may be back in business.

Culture

The news media are not the only ones trying to tell us about our world, of course: beyond the news is "culture" – books, theatre, music, film, art, TV, whatever presents a kind of mediated image of our society. Can you use this to campaign? Well, it's been done. Charles Kingsley's The Water Babies, published in 1862, shocked the Victorians with its tragic tale of a young chimney sweep who drowns after being chased out of an upper-class home, and within a year of its publication parliament had made it illegal to send small boys up chimneys. Cathy Come Home, a drama about homelessness aired by the BBC in 1966, provoked both public outrage and the founding of Shelter. More recently, Morgan Spurlock's film Super Size Me drew widespread attention to the horrors of a diet based entirely on McDonald's; by an amazing coincidence the fast food firm has since revamped both its food and its image. And there is a long list of novels and plays that have prompted change or inspired activists, from feminist set texts such as Marilyn French's The Women's Room to David Hare's drama about rail privatisation, The Permanent Way.

These come from exceptionally talented individuals, however. I do not wish to be rude, but the chances that you have a Charles Kingsley or a David Hare in your organisation are quite small. When lesser minds attempt to combine politics and art, the result is often the most fatally pretentious bullshit you can possibly imagine.

Still, if you simply can't resist the temptation, your best bet is probably what is known as cultural activism or culture jamming – going toe to toe with the corporations on their own territory, by wittily defacing billboards, say, or kneeling to worship chickens in Asda. This kind of mickey-taking is something Americans have long excelled at, particularly in the form of satirical magazines, from Ballyhoo in the 1930s through Mad and Spy to the online Onion. The Reverend Billy ("He puts the odd back in God!") is a master of the wind-up: he's been running an anti-consumer campaign in the States for several years now, holding prayer meetings in Starbucks, celebrating No Shopping Day every November, performing with his Stop Shopping gospel choir.

I'm not convinced that cultural activism alone changes governments' minds, or engages corporations: the "insurrectionary imagination", as the cultural activist Jennifer Verson describes it, is just too remote from the way most big organisations think. Culture jamming can be little more than a nuisance or, even worse, yet another "ironic" sales technique for the crafty corporation. Rev Billy's sermons are very good, his campaign is wonderful, but it is a big in-joke: you only get it if you already agree with what he is saying. And that is true of most cultural activism: its usefulness lies mainly in giving other activists a good laugh. When the Laboratory of the Insurrectionary Imagination managed to close down Selfridges for an hour in 2004 by praying loudly, in various locations around to the store, to the God of Immaculate Consumption, it left all kinds of activists with smiles on their faces. It was good for morale, and that in itself is a worthwhile end. But it was never going to change the world.

The personal approach

So far we've talked about spreading your message through the organised media. But just think how much of your information comes from interaction with other people: talking to a friend on the phone, or having a conversation at the school gates, or logging on to an internet chatroom. As the phenomenon of the viral email has shown in recent years, a message given to one person, if "sticky" enough, can spread around the world in a shockingly brief time.

The term "stickiness" comes from Malcolm Gladwell's book The Tipping Point, which gives as an example the famous ride of the American revolutionary Paul Revere, who discovered in 1775 that the British were going to crack down on the colonial rebels. Revere rode out of Boston at midnight, and within two hours had managed to reach 13 nearby towns, rouse local leaders and get them to send out messengers of their own. "When the British finally began their march towards Lexington on the morning of the 19th, their foray into the countryside was met – to their utter astonishment – with organised and fierce resistance." Gladwell continues the story with a fascinating examination of why Revere was the best possible man for this job because of his exceptional social skills. But the story's power comes from that human ability to construct networks where moments ago there was nothing.

For the past decade or so marketeers and campaigners (funnily enough, the two groups often cross over) have been increasingly trying to exploit this ability. "Social marketing", as they call it, shuns big ad campaigns in favour of a series of small-scale events; Patrick Butler, editor of the Guardian's society, health and education policy, likens it to a book that is published without much publicity, but, through word of mouth, becomes a huge hit. "It comes from below, instead of from on top, in other words." This, however, is what the most savvy small campaign groups have been doing for years anyway. Take the Fabians: formed in 1884, they became one of the most important powerhouses of leftwing thought in Britain. They were clear from early on that their aims were to work for gradual political change (one contemporary described their philosophy as "Don't be in a hurry; but when you do go it, go it Thick!"). They would look into social conditions and publish the results and their conclusions, and organise public lecture tours where their members could enlighten people about socialism. They were one of the very first political thinktanks, and they were immediately, enormously in demand.

The tours sold out, their books were bestsellers, and around the country Fabian societies sprang up like weeds. People had to be turned away in huge crowds from Annie Besant's lectures, and George Bernard Shaw became one of the most regular lecturers of all: between 1883 and 1895, with virtually no exceptions, he delivered one or even two lectures every Sunday, and plenty on weekdays too. This work turned out to be invaluable a few years later when the Labour party was putting up its first candidates: the ideas were already in general circulation.

So forget the huge poster campaign. Put a funny video on YouTube. Stick fake parking tickets on 4x4s to protest at their high fuel use. Set up a Facebook group. Give a brilliant interview on a community radio station. Make a speech at your local school. Ask your local council to take part in a special day to promote your cause. Take a green show on tour around the country. Social marketing – or campaigning – is about building a solid base of support. It's about travelling from meeting to meeting, talking to people endlessly, sending out mailouts, having discussions with outreach projects, targeting different sections of society rather than trying to splat everyone at once. It's about generally putting yourself about personally rather than counting on the mass media to do it. So if you do decide that you want to concentrate your efforts on communicating with the public about your issues, this is the way to go: it's certainly more affordable, however clearly that TV ad may sing in your mind's eye. Halt! Do not attempt to book that slot! It's a waste of your time and money.

The law and ... defamation

First the good news. Thanks to a 1993 ruling by the House of Lords, you can say or print anything you like about central or local government (although you still have to be careful – if your remarks reflect badly on specific government officers or councillors they may decide to sue you privately) without the risk of being sued for defamation. You can also say anything you want about the dead, as long as you don't implicate anyone living with what you say.

Now the bad: if you say or write anything that damages anyone else's reputation, whether it's a living person or an organisation, and you can't stand up your remarks, you can be sued and left without a brass button to your name. Some companies will reach for their lawyers at the slightest provocation, even when it doesn't bring them any benefit, although the long, high-profile McLibel case should have shown them the terrible PR that can result from taking a small campaign group to court. And if you want to fight the case, you'll probably have to either pay for it yourself or conduct it yourself. Legal aid is not available for slander (defamation by speech) or libel (defamation in writing or broadcast form – anything published in permanent form really), although it can be for malicious falsehood.

How does a court decide if something is defamatory? By considering two questions: is the natural and ordinary meaning of the words defamatory; or is there any innuendo in them? To put it another way, could readers or viewers (it almost always is readers, since libel suits far exceed slander) reasonably extract a defamatory meaning from the words by "reading between the lines"?

The company or person suing you needs to prove two more things in order to win. Firstly that the material was published by you. Now publication is defined very broadly to mean any communication to another person (although English and Scots law differs here. In England, publication must be to someone other than the claimant, but in Scotland, even a communication of the statement to the claimant can constitute defamation. In other words you can be sued for writing someone a nasty letter). Potentially, anyone involved in the distribution of an allegation can be responsible for publication even if their involvement is small, although there are some exceptions for distributors. The important thing is that 'publication' doesn't just apply to media organisations: it can mean you as well. Secondly the litigants need to prove that the statement referred to the company or person either by name or by any other means that would allow some readers to identify it.

The best thing, of course, is to avoid finding yourself in court in the first place. Make sure that any statements you make are backed up with fact. You should have at least one good, reliable source for any negative claims you make. If you are just repeating something you've heard elsewhere, try to find out what it's based on. This is basic common sense for a campaign anyway: it gives campaigning a bad name if everyone just repeats the same old stuff without actually checking to see if it's true. Obviously that's difficult if you're dealing with a multinational company's transgressions abroad, say. But if you are not sure in your own mind that these things have actually occurred, how can you campaign on them? A few phone calls, some research online and you may be able to back up your case beautifully.

But if the worst comes to the worst, how can you defend yourself? There are a number of defences available:

Justification: If the statement you have made is proven to be true, then the action against you will fail. However, the onus is on you to prove the statement's truth: unusually the law of libel assumes a statement is false once the claimant has shown that it has been published, is defamatory, and that he or she is identified. The test is "on the balance of probabilities" rather than "beyond reasonable doubt".

Fair comment: If your statement is an expression of opinion on a matter of public interest, this defence may succeed. But you must also show that your statement is the expression of an opinion, not an allegation of fact, that it is based on true facts contained or referred to in the publication, and that it is made without malice, and that you genuinely believe what you have said.

Privilege: There are certain kinds of statements which can claim a "privileged" status: it's a sort of immunity from being sued. Statements made in court or in parliament are protected by "absolute privilege" and are not actionable in defamation, even if they are made maliciously. Slightly below "absolute privilege" is "qualified privilege": these types of statements are protected from an defamation action if they are made on the basis of a properly founded belief in their truth, but not if they are made maliciously, either knowing them to be untrue or not caring whether they are true or false. A statement made by someone who has a duty to communicate it, to someone with an interest in receiving it, may fall under this category – for example, passing on employment references or crime reports to the police. But the most complex type of "qualified privilege" applies to media reports: they need to prove that they are on a subject of public interest and have complied with the standards of responsible journalism, as defined by the courts.

Meanwhile, if you think that you may not be able to win the case, you can make an **offer of amends**: say you'll publish a suitable correction and sufficient apology and pay the claimant compensation and costs. (If the person suing you rejects this offer, this will constitute a defence for you, unless they can prove that it wasn't just all a mistake and you were deliberately setting out to smear them.)

What happens if you lose? The court will slap an injunction on the material, which means you can't repeat the offending remarks.

It may also award damages to your opponent to compensate them for any financial injury caused by the libel. There's no telling how much that might be: most libel cases are tried by a judge and jury, with the jury deciding who wins and awarding damages to the successful claimant. As a result it depends very much on the lawyers or the jury or the weather that morning. Costs are awarded to the winner and these days they can easily outstrip any award of damages. In addition, lawyers acting for claimants suing on a conditional fee arrangement can double their fees if they win, in theory to compensate them for the risk they took in taking on the case.

By the way, remember that if you're running a website, you could be sued for any defamatory comments posted by users, as you are likely to be held to have published them by allowing them to be posted. It's still unclear how this works, and on one of the few occasions where it has actually happened – when "baby guru" Gina Ford sued Mumsnet for comments made about her in the website's forum – the case was settled before reaching court with an apology and a promise that there would be no further discussion of Ford on the site. But the owner of Mumsnet subsequently commented that the decision to settle was taken "at least in part because of the distinct lack of clarity about how the defamation law applies to web forums". The law is now being clarified in this area.

Chapter Twelve
Going into politics

Of course there is one obvious way to make an impact, and I'm surprised more campaigners don't try it. Set up your own political party, win the general election, take over the country and do it all the right way. Especially since, as it turns out, it's very easy to register your own party. Ever since the Electoral Commission was set up in 2001, all you have to do is submit a cheque for £150, a constitution (stating your aims and policies), a financial plan and a completed form RP1 UK, RP1 GB or RP1 NI, all of which can be downloaded from the Electoral Commission website. But you're in shark-infested waters even before you go head to head with Labour or the DUP: the competition is intense, with another 400 political parties already registered (who knew?) on the website.

Most have got emblems – however terrible. The Independence Index, for example, has a pen drawing of a cat. The Telepathic Partnership of Reading, has an emblem that states You ♥ Me. The Rock'n'Roll Loony party has a cat holding a guitar. The Space Navies party, registered in 2006, has the old illuminati pyramid/eye thing going on. There are many socialist parties, a lot of People's parties, loads of Independent parties, but also several single-issue parties, such as Save Chase Farm and Save Bristol North Baths, while I fancy the Red and Green Alliance party. I was also instantly drawn to the Had Enough party, whose emblem reads simply: "Have you had enough?"

There was a number on its website, so I rang up and a woman answered. I asked for the Had Enough party, and she said, "George is not here at the moment. Will you call back in an hour or so?"

When I rang again, this time George answered and was kind enough to explain how it all came about. "Basically I started the party because I'd had enough of our local politicians – the MEPs, the MPs – who act, I think, with arrogance and disrespect. They're not interested in your problem. They're in it solely for the money and the perks, and I thought it was time for someone to start complaining." The website is pretty clear: George has Had Enough "of private sector workers being discriminated against by the government", "of government spin (We are winning the war in Iraq)", "of the House of Lords (stop this abusive waste of privilege", and "of MPs and MEPs claiming over-excessive expenses".

He's a printer, it turns out, and you'd think this would be handy because one of the biggest costs of any election campaign is printing. But he says not really: "I still have to buy paper. We set up in September 2006. The Electoral Commission were not very helpful; they do make it hard for you to set up your own political party. There are so many forms you have to fill in, and every three months you have to send information about donations, expenses, everything. You literally get bumf every week. It's a lot of work for a small political party."

He lives in Penicuik, in the Midlothian district of Scotland, and he ran in the May 2007 Scottish elections. "The biggest problem we had is that the media are so politically biased – they don't give you any coverage if you don't belong to one of the big parties. The BBC are the worst – I got no airtime at all, which makes it so hard. You have to be like Tommy Sheridan [the Scottish socialist politician] and do something outrageous; if you're a normal person trying they're just not interested. A lot of people asked me why I was standing – they said all I'd do would be split the vote. I printed out 38,000 leaflets and got them out all round the constituency, and that cost about £600, just the paper alone, and then it was £500 to register for the election."

With all these problems, why did he do it? "Oh, we had brilliant fun. The best fun we had was sticking it right up the politicians. Everywhere I went I left them my card. I went on the hustings, too;

I spoke for about 10 to 15 minutes, did myself quite proud. Most of the politicians have just got their heads up their bum – they've lost touch with normal people, they just make up stuff to tell them." Why did he start his own party and not just stand as an independent candidate? "Well, if I had run as an independent I wouldn't have been able to have my catchphrase, something that people remembered. I ended up getting 680 votes, which I think is not that bad. A lot of the independents didn't get any votes at all." His voice is full of glee, and he definitely plans to run again. The politics bug has well and truly bitten George McCleery.

Other than the chance to use your catchphrase, is there really any point in forming your own political party? How much impact can you have: what will happen when your shiny boat of ideals crashes up against the black cliffs of politics? It's interesting to contemplate what's happened to the Labour Party, so new and idealistic back in 1893 under the leadership of the legendary Keir Hardie. Hardie already had a seat in Parliament when the Independent Labour Party was formed, he had astounded Parliament a year earlier by taking his seat as the country's first Socialist MP wearing his famous bristling beard, a tweed jacket and a deerstalker hat. What kind of world did he and his party face? The old social contracts had been torn up throughout the West, but particularly in Britain: God or the Monarch was no longer in charge, so this was an interesting new universe where politicans, businessmen and lawyers would be in charge of the way we lived. The twentieth century around the world, as a result, has been a political laboratory in which every idea has been subjected to painful and humiliating experiments. Fascism, totalitarianism, communism, socialism, fundamentalism: you name it, someone has tried it, (as Winston Churchill once said: "Democracy is the worst system apart from all the others") while during the last couple of decades the free marketeers and bankers have been ascendant, slowly capturing every port (whether the coming recession will alter this we will find out).

Paul Foot pinned down the moment where socialism butted right up against capitalism, and lost: Labour had confidently won the election of 1964, but inherited a huge deficit of payments from the Tories: they were immediately forced to shelve half their election promises in order to keep the situation stable. But the head of the Bank of England, Lord Cromer, wanted more: he wanted "a wage freeze, cuts in public spending and a rise in unemployment", as well as a sharp rise in the borrowing rate. Foot quotes Wilson's description of his confrontation with Cromer on the evening after he had won his rise (at this point the government still controlled bank rates): "I said that we had now reached the situation where a newly elected Government with a mandate from the people was being told, not so much by the Governor of the Bank of England but by international speculators, that the policies on which we had fought the election could not be implemented; that the Government was to be forced into the adoption of Tory policies to which it was fundamentally opposed. The Governor confirmed that that was in fact the case ... I asked him if this meant that it was impossible for any government, whatever its party label, whatever its manifesto or the policies on which it fought an election, to continue, unless it immediately reverted to full-scale Tory policies. He had to admit that that was what his argument meant, because of the sheer compulsion of the economic dictation of those who exercised economic power." That was it for the UK at least: Socialist ideas had penetrated right into Downing Street, right into the seat of power, only to be told they were not welcome. Bang crash went the shiny boat on those cruel sharp rocks.

Labour's first manifesto, 1900
- Adequate maintenance from national funds for the aged poor
- Public provision of better houses for the people
- Useful work for the unemployed
- Adequate maintenance for children
- No compulsory vaccination
- Public control of the liquor traffic
- Nationalisation of land and railways
- Relief of local rates by grants from the national exchequer
- Legislative independence for all parts of the empire
- Abolition of the standing army, and the establishment of a citizen force
- The people to decide on peace or war
- Graduated income tax
- Shorter parliaments
- Adult suffrage
- Registration reform
- Payment of members

"The object of these measures is to enable the people ultimately to obtain the socialisation of the means of production, distribution and exchange, to be controlled by a democratic state in the interests of the entire community, and the complete emancipation of labour from the domination of capitalism and landlordism, with the establishment of social and economic equality between the sexes."

And the problems may not just come from outside. What about Respect, another party that set out to break the mould. The name stood for Respect Equality Socialism Peace Environment Community Trade Unionism, but just as important as all these fine aspirations was its goal of giving British Muslims a political voice. I met one of its young activists at a union rally; she was a Muslim girl with her head uncovered, about 18, full of idealism and socialist ideals, who genuinely believed that Respect could be the future for her and her friends and family.

After about three minutes of Everything Being Beautiful, however, Everything Turned Ugly. Within a month of Respect's launch in January 2004, one of the founder members, George Monbiot, had pulled out because it was clashing with the Green party. The general election campaign that followed, with Respect's troublesome figurehead George Galloway (newly chucked out of the Labour party) up against Oona King in London's Bethnal Green, was absolutely poisonous, with accusations of bullying being flung around. King's car had eggs thrown at it; Galloway received death threats. He won, however, and Respect picked up a good handful of council seats. But the cracks soon reopened. I spoke to another of Respect's early members, then former football club chairman Kris Stewart, in the summer of 2007, and he was already unhappy with the way things were going. "We've got lots of people who are not really sure what Respect is supposed to be," he told me, "and it's not clear to me what Respect might be in a year's time." The difficulty of holding together a party that housed both Islamists and progressive socialists – with their very different views on women, gay rights, etc – were already becoming clear. Four councillors in Tower Hamlets resigned the Respect whip in order to become independents, citing the party's "undemocratic" workings. Then Galloway delivered a letter of criticism to the Respect head of 27 committee, and shortly after that, according to members of Respect, he entered the HQ with colleagues one night and changed all the locks. Galloway's spokesman said that the locks were changed because "the parliamentary rules in terms of financing insist that the office can only be a constituency office for the MP and it cannot be a party political office". He has now announced plans to stand for election as Respect MP in the constituency of Poplar and Limehouse, if the general election ever happens. That will definitely be one to watch.

Still want to form your own party? Thought not. How about running as an independent MP? You'll still have your work cut out: there have only ever been a teeny handful of independents in the Commons, and most have got there for unique local reasons, such as the former BBC man Martin Bell, who in 1997 became the first independent MP for nearly 50 years on the back of popular disgust at Tatton's Tory incumbent, Neil Hamilton. Both Labour and the Lib Dems withdrew from the race to give him a clear run. Dai Davies, the self-styled "hairy-arsed steel worker" from the "socialist republic of Blaenau Gwent", would probably not have made it to Westminster as an independent member of parliament if Labour hadn't infuriated the constituency by parachuting in an unpopular candidate in the 2005 general election.

Ralph Nader, the independent's independent

Ralph Nader is one of the most famous independent political candidates ever. He has run for the US presidency five times: the first time not on the ballot sheet but as a name you could write in the box marked "None of the above", the second and third times for the Green party, and the last couple of times as an independent. Nader is one of my heroes: he has the combination of idealism, integrity, passion for justice and dug-in bloody-mindedness that makes the perfect campaigner. He first made an impact back in the 50s when he exposed the car manufacturers that were avoiding incorporating safety measures into their vehicles because of the expense; General Motors was so furious it put a private detective on to him. His private life, however, was squeeky clean. He sued GM for harassment, won, and used the money to get together a group of young investigators who became known as Nader's Raiders.

On not very much sleep and large quantities of coffee, the Raiders took on institution after institution, and Nader's standing

---

with the public meant the reports were listened to by the government. During the 60s and 70s he got the law changed on issues like seatbelts and airbags, food labelling, air quality, the right to know if you're being exposed to toxic chemicals at work, nicotine labelling on cigarettes, warnings on pharmaceutical packaging, and dozens of other issues. And then Reagan arrived, the door was shut in Nader's face, and the corporations began to wind the clock back.

But his capital with ordinary Americans remained high: he was perceived as (and clearly is) a man of integrity (Newsweek put him on their cover in a suit of armour, for God's sake!). When he decided to run for president in 2000 with the aim of exposing the corruption and dead wood at the heart of the US electoral system, supporters flocked to him. He played one sold-out venue after another, with the highlight a date at Madison Square Gardens where he was supported by Susan Sarandon, Michael Moore, Bill Murray and Patti Smith; thousands cheered wildly for his plans to challenge corporate power, to talk about global citizenship instead of global markets.

"Ralph Nader is the best American I know," said Bill Murray afterwards. The media ignored him almost completely, but the supporters were having a ball. And then they got to Florida, where Nader picked up 96,000 votes and Al Gore lost by 60, and ... Nader's name became dirt. His decision to run again in the 2004 election was greeted with howls of derision: Michael Moore went on his knees to Nader on TV to beg him to keep out, and Jimmy Carter, once a fan, advised him to go back to "examining the rear end of automobiles". The Democrats lost again, although at least this time, given his 0.38 per cent of the vote, no one could blame Nader.

Nader's once high reputation has suffered tremendously. Former supporters have turned against him, the head of one of the organisations he set up – Public Citizen – wanted to take his name off its letterhead, and one of Nader's former Raiders said his kids now tease him that he worked for "that crazy guy". Now this is why I really love Nader: in February 2008 he announced that he was again running as an independent.

"I don't care about my legacy," he told the film-makers Henriette Mantel and Steve Skrovan, who made a film about him last year called An Unreasonable Man. "I care about how much justice is advanced in America and in our world day after day. And I'm willing to advance whatever quote 'reputation' I have in the cause of that effort."

Have Nader's attempts to become president improved the world, or furthered any of the causes he holds dear? He hasn't made it into office, and has probably lost much of the standing that made him such an effective advocate for consumers. There has been no deep soul-searching in America about the value of an electoral system where candidates congregate in the middle ground and anyone who steps outside can be pilloried as Nader has been. But all the same, for some reason it feels like a good thing to have done.

Now he is an MP, Davies doesn't present an entirely attractive picture of his job. "In terms of the place itself," he says, "it's barking mad. I stood in the lobby one night, and there were government ministers asking if they're standing in the right place. The other problem is that as an MP most of your work is from other people failing to do what they should. Seventy per cent of my work is spent covering omissions by local councils, the police, the health service: only 30 is spent making representations to ministers and that sort of thing. They do talk to backbenchers, they do respond – I've been impressed by that. They are trying to improve the role of the back-bencher. But a lot of the time backbenchers are just voting fodder."

In real terms, however, Davies can have as much impact as any ordinary MP: he can put down amendments, early day motions and private members' bills (see Lobbying for more details of what an MP can do). If you're serious about this then you need to look at the Electoral Commission website which has detailed factsheets about the procedure you need to follow. You need to be over 18, and either a British citizen, a citizen of the Republic of Ireland or a citizen of a Commonwealth country which does not require leave to enter or remain in the UK. There is a long list of disqualifications which you'll need to go through to make sure that you are not included.

Then wait till parliament dissolves, and submit a completed set of nomination forms along with a £500 deposit to the returning officer in your constituency – your local Commission office will be able to tell you how to contact them. You'll need to fill in a nomination paper, which must have 10 signatures from the constituency supporting your candidacy; a home address form and a form giving your consent to nomination.

But really, unless you can persuade the big parties to step aside at the next election, you may have to aim a little lower than the Commons. There is another option however; I don't think many activists really take local councils seriously enough but these organisations are directly in charge of an extraordinary proportion of our lives. They regulate our schools, our local shops and bars; they're responsible for most planning decisions, for social housing and libraries, for parking and all our waste. And becoming a local councillor, whether as an independent or with one of the parties, is far easier than becoming an MP. Once again, you should look at the Electoral Commission website, which contains information about how to stand for a local council. You should also:

Check that you are eligible and then **register as a candidate** by contacting the returning officer at your local authority and asking for registration forms and guidance for candidates. Make sure you get the forms back at least seven days before the deadline, in case you've made a mistake that needs to be corrected.

Register an election agent. This can be a mate, or you can even do it yourself. Their job is to run your campaign. Their office (which can be their home) must either be in the same area as you or nearby; check the regulations for your area. Their name and address, and that of the printer, must appear on all election literature, or you could be fined up to £5,000. Email addresses are not enough.

Decide your budget and keep a record of all your expenses; this is a legal requirement. For simplicity's sake, you may decide that your agent will handle all expenses.

Set up a group to help you with leafleting and canvassing, if you don't already have support in place. It's illegal to pay your canvassers, by the way.

Choose your methods of communication and decide what you want to say. Your options, more or less, are leafleting, door-todoor canvassing and press. A well-presented leaflet can be an effective introduction.

While you're out canvassing, you can offer lifts to the polling station; on election day this may end up being an important part of your day. You're allowed to attend the count with your election agent and another person of your choice. If you win, remember to sign your declaration of acceptance of office. You must, whatever the outcome, submit a return detailing your election expenses.

It's worth remembering that whether you get in or not, just standing can have an impact. Jo Offer stood as an independent in the Brighton & Hove elections after a year of campaigning about a dump that the council was planning to site near a local school. "I didn't want to get voted in," she says. "I did it because I just had no one to vote for. We managed to get manifestos out, so more people could understand what we were standing for, and that was useful in terms of publicising the campaign. But it was also helpful because it meant that the Labour and Green candidates had to actually talk about the issue."

She enjoyed it, although it was a very "exposing experience". And independent councillors generally are a force to be reckoned with: there's even one council in Boston, Lincolnshire, that is controlled by the Boston Bypass party, which is campaigning for the bypass they say the town desperately needs.

In short, if you want to be more involved in your community and have a direct impact on people's lives, your local council is a good start. If, however, you want to influence the government's policies, there are far simpler and more effective ways than going into politics yourself.

Chapter Thirteen
Legal action

It's no accident that in films lawyers are always surrounded by huge leather-bound books with teeny-weeny print inside. They need them. UK law, European law, international law are all leafed in ever-widening circles of ferocious, bewildering complexity, so fiendishly interwoven that no one, apart from lawyers (and often not even them), really understands the whole thing. Even apparently simple questions such as, "Is that civil law, public law or criminal law?" may lead to a long pause and the sound of flying pages. It's a crazy system.

But it's right that it should be crazy. In the 20th and 21st centuries particularly, as the influence of religion has faded, the law has increasingly been called upon to decide what is right and what is wrong.

And that is a very complicated judgment, subject to the pressure of circumstance, contemporary mores and even (though this should not be so) finance.

Basically, we're governed by three layers of law. The top layer, and the furthest away, is decided by international agreements, such as the UN's Universal Declaration on Human Rights, or the Organisation for Economic Co-operation and Development's (OECD) guidelines for multinational enterprises. These are only legally binding to the extent that countries have signed up for them. And they're only binding on governments, not their corporations or inhabitants. With the OECD guidelines, for example, the British government has a duty to create a central reporting system. But companies have no legal obligation to comply with the guidelines:

the government can only point out breaches and suggest improvements.

The middle layer, as far as the UK is concerned, is European legislation, which comes in two main flavours. There are EU laws, which are just straightforward laws, passed by the European parliament and the Council of Ministers and applicable throughout the EU, and then there are EU directives, which countries are supposed to incorporate into their own legal systems, although this can take quite a long time, the UK being particularly slow about sorting out some of the environmental directives.

And the bottom layer is our own domestic law, a combination of statute law (all the laws that parliament has passed) and common law (the mass of court rulings considered to be "precedents", which influence decisions in subsequent cases). It's messy and fearsomely difficult, but it does allow for the oddities and exceptions that are part of life. As one solicitor told me, "Basically, judges make it up as they go along." For some reason I find that reassuring.

With the help of some very kind experts (Phil McLeish, Ben Silverstone, Susanna Rickard and Sean Humber) I've compiled the following list of possible lines of attack if you want to take on the government or the corporations legally.

Challenge the corporations

As I said at the beginning of this book, corporate accountability is one of the most important issues in the modern world, and the international community is increasingly making noises about ways of enforcing it. And if you're up against the corporations, legal action is potentially one of the most powerful options. For a start, you can get directors into court, under oath, and ask them questions about the way they do business. You can demand to see all their documents on a certain subject. You can potentially force them to reveal, then change, the way they operate. The law, after all, is the only power that corporations recognise as greater than their duty to maximise profits.

However, there are serious problems involved in going down this route. Firstly, it's prohibitively expensive. It's expensive anywhere in the world, but in the UK the loser in a civil case must usually pay the winner's expenses. If you're considering a fairly risky case – suing a company for negligence, perhaps – the possibility that you may end up paying the ginormous amounts that the company involved will spend to defend itself is pretty daunting. This, of course, hugely restricts our access to justice, to say nothing of our ability to expose shameful behaviour: while a megacorp can afford to sue all and sundry, for most individuals or small campaign groups a defamation case would be ruinously expensive. The human rights lawyer Keir Starmer believes this imbalance creates a "real risk" that criticism will be stifled.

Secondly, legal action can go on for years. And years. Round one in your local court, round two in the high court, round three in the court of appeal, round four in the European court, "as two spent swimmers that do cling together and choke their art". (In McLibel, in which two campaigners were accused of defaming McDonald's, writs were issued by the corporation in September 1990, but it was not until June 1997 that Mr Justice Bell finally ruled on the case. It then rolled around the European courts for another eight years. Yes, that was one of the longest trials in history. But you never know – yours could top it.)

Thirdly, it involves a huge amount of work. You can't just sue a company for being a Very Naughty Corporation. You have to come up with a case. You have to prove it. You have to read through the 10bn tons of paperwork that will be dumped on your head. Sure, you can leave some of this to your lawyer, but there will still be plenty for you to be getting on with.

Fourthly, let's be honest here – your chances of success are fairly low. Courts are known, on the whole, to be conservative: they do not want to alter the status quo unless forced to. And because the law in this country draws so heavily on precedent, if your case goes wrong you may even end up damaging your cause by making future actions even harder to win. If you lose the case, you risk the whole issue. I asked the human rights lawyer Peter Roderick if he could think of any landmark cases that had forced a company to seriously rethink its policies and there was a long, long pause, before he suggested asbestos. (A battle that went on, I have read, for a hundred years. Which makes McLibel look like a weekend in Paris.)

But perhaps you're a carefree billionaire with a burning sense of natural justice? In that case, step this way.

Civil liability gives someone who has suffered as a result of another person or company's actions the right to redress. (Simply being outraged doesn't count, by the way.) Recent cases have established that a company can be sued in its home jurisdiction for its actions abroad, so cases can be brought here on behalf of workers in, say, Burma. There are a number of ways of taking action that I'll just glance at.

Personal injury cases have come to be seen as a bad thing, leading to all sorts of elf'n'safety nonsense. But it's vital to remember that they started life as a way for David to take on Goliath, where individuals tried to hold corporations responsible for ruining their lives. John Edwards, who has twice run for US president, made his millions and his name as a champion of the underdog, winning hundreds of personal injury suits – most famously a $25m suit against the manufacturer of a defective pool drain cover after a three-year-old girl was disembowelled in a horrible accident although damages are usually higher in the US.

Such suits could be powerful tools where the pollution created by companies has caused physical harm. They could also be used when companies have been careless with radiation, sewage, industrial waste or pesticides, but "causation" – that the company was responsible, and that the material caused harm – must be shown, and that is a big stumbling block. As any environmental lawyer will tell you (with a certain amount of bitterness) courts are reluctant to get involved in scientific issues, so unless the link between the substance and the harm is already well established, they may rule against you.

Nuisance cases are brought where you can establish that there has been "unlawful interference with a person's use of or enjoyment of land". They're not used very often, and are generally thought of as being for rich neighbours who want to bicker about their hedges. But they might be possible if you were bothered by smells from a nearby waste facility or factory, or kept awake by noise. In some ways these suits have been supplanted by Article 8 of the Human Rights Act, which states that everyone is entitled to respect for "his private and family life, his home and his correspondence". However, they have a longer history, so in some cases they may be a safer bet. **Loss and damage suits** usually apply to the devaluation of property by stuff like toxic waste, methane leaks, noise, radiation and emissions from local industry. This last area could be of interest to, for example, a community living near an incinerator or a pesticide plant.

The Alien Tort Claims Act (ATCA – also sometimes referred to as the Alien Tort Statute) is an interesting recent development in the States. It's actually a very old US statute, first enacted in 1789, but no one paid it much attention until it was rediscovered by a clever lawyer in the 1970s. It is now starting to have a real impact in the States. It permits victims to sue for a civil wrong "committed in violation of the law of nations", and was used by Burmese villagers who accused the US oil company Unocal of using enforced labour during the building of a pipeline; the company settled in 2004. In 2007 Yahoo! settled another case brought on behalf of a Chinese dissident who alleged that the internet company had passed information about him to the Chinese government, which had led to his arrest. In February 2008 the US justice department asked the supreme court to dismiss a fascinating case under ATCA against a group of multinationals including Deutsche Bank, Barclays, GM Motors, IBM and Exxon Mobil, among others, for collaborating with the South African government to maintain apartheid. The US government claimed that it would bring about a "dramatic expansion" of US law, particularly the use of ATCA. The case was still under consideration as this book went to press but attorney Paul Hoffman, heading the apartheid case, says: "The reason we're doing this is because there is no other form of international regulation which allows us to hold corporations accountable." One case at a time like this is not ideal, but it's a start, he thinks.

The lawyers have yet to win a ATCA case against a corporation (so far it has been most successful against torturers), but businesses are feeling the heat. There is much discussion of putting human rights agreements in place within corporations, and with partners and even foreign governments if the company is working abroad. Cases can only be brought in US courts, against companies or individuals within US jurisdiction, but they can be brought in connection with activities round the world. It is only a start, but it is that.

Why I fight

Charlie Hopkins
Environmental lawyer

The frustrating thing about this job, and something I'm seeing more and more, is that we'll win the public inquiry and then the decision will be overturned by the government. As one QC put it to me: "Sometimes I really don't know why we effing bother."

I started off as a geographer, and then trained in law when I was 35. I'd got to know some people at the "radical bar", barristers doing work that had a certain political consciousness about it. There wasn't a great deal of environmental legal work going on in the late 80s, but I thought that there was scope for an environmental practice. By this time there was growing consciousness of environmental issues, centred around things like Sellafield, the Camelford incident, the growing number of incinerators coming on stream, discharging who knows what into the local communities' air, the quality of sea water ... a whole range of things. By the 90s, legal action had come to be perceived as another angle

---

to campaigning, and some of the work I did with Surfers Against Sewage was really exciting. But I was getting frustrated, so in 1997 I left the legal firm I'd been working for and set up the Earthrights practice, which is probably one of the only legal firms in the UK devoted entirely to environmental law.

There's very little money in environmental law, it must be said, and it's getting harder and harder to get cases to court. But there's such satisfaction in representing people whose voices would otherwise not be heard. Frustration and satisfaction in equal parts.

Use the public authorities

But wait, you're saying. I feel robbed! That last section was so short! Is that all there is? No, but the other way of bringing corporations to heel is quite pleasing because you basically get the government or the judiciary or the police to take on most of the expense and administration. In order to do this, however, you will have to demonstrate some kind of case against the corporation, so you need to familiarise yourself with the law relevant to your area of interest. It sounds daunting, and it may take a little while, but you just need an internet connection and some ProPlus. Then:

Contact the police. They don't spend all their time shooting Brazilian electricians, you know. In 2001 Warwickshire police force announced proudly that it had appointed the country's first environmental crime officer, for example, and other constabularies have followed suit. Kent's rural and environmental crime co-ordinator apparently deals with "heritage crime, wildlife issues, environmental crime and Dave the dolphin". (I'm afraid I didn't find out what Dave had been getting up to).

Environmental crime is a particularly interesting area of law at the moment. The House of Commons' environmental audit committee got interested in the subject in 2003 and produced a very helpful report that pointed out, among other things, that under the

Environmental Protection Act 1990 (EPA) pollution equals "substances which are capable of causing harm to man or any other living organisms supported by the environment". Which certainly opens up a few possibilities: carbon emissions would certainly come into that category, for a start. Our environmental law is increasingly defined by EU directives, and in early 2007 the European Commission put out a draft directive that would require member states to treat breaches of environmental law as criminal offences. A directive on environmental liability that means polluters will be liable for damage to the environment is slowly, slowly being incorporated into UK law; that too opens up some interesting possibilities for prosecution.

Corporations can also be found guilty of the same crimes as people – manslaughter, for example. In the past, the prosecution had to prove the gross negligence of one person who was the embodiment of the company; cases such as that following the Zeebrugge disaster showed the near-impossibility of doing this. But now it needs to be proved only that the company was organised in a way that led to the death in question. Still quite tough to do, but faintly possible.

Bringing a case will require a bit of nerve. But some sections of the police force – as we've seen with the investigations into Labour party high-ups over funding – are more up for taking on big organisations than they used to be. And they will hopefully decide, at the very least, to pay the company in question a visit, which has to be worth something. Make sure you alert the local press. If you find it impossible to get the police interested, you could launch a private prosecution – but this can be horribly expensive, and the state can take over and then abandon the case at any time.

Contact your local council. The local authority is the body that deals with statutory nuisance (see above), as well as noise pollution and pollution pollution. It's required to act against local organisations that are breaching the EPA.

Contact the Health and Safety Executive. These are the people to talk to if you think your employer has not been fulfilling its health and safety requirements.

Get in touch with the OECD's national contact point. The national contact point (NCP) is obliged by law to investigate breaches of the OECD's guidelines for multinational enterprises, which stipulate, for example, that corporations "should contribute to the effective abolition of child labour" and the "wider goals of sustainable development". If the NCP thinks there is some basis to your complaint, and the company does not satisfy the NCP that it will deal with the issue, the NCP will put out recommendations for change. In other words, it will name and shame, baby. Norway's NCP, which operates by the same rules, investigated a company that had been helping to maintain the prison at Guantánamo Bay; it ended up publicly urging the company to undertake a thorough assessment of the ethical issues raised by its contractual relationships.

Before you get too excited, the UK has looked at just a dozen or so cases since 2000, and in 2006 the government was given a bit of a kicking by NGOs complaining that its reports on the breaches were useless. They were often unclear and, as the human rights lawyer Daniel Leader pointed out to me, didn't even appear to reach a conclusion about whether the rules had been broken or not. The government promised to shape up, enlarged the NCP and now refers to it as one of its principal instruments for bolstering corporate responsibility. It remains to be seen how that will translate into action.

Challenge the public authorities

Finally, you can fight the decisions that public authorities have made. Americans are particularly strong on this. Back in the 60s the Sierra Club, a fairly wealthy conservation group, started legal action against Walt Disney, which was planning to turn a lovely valley into a ski resort; that action led to the formation of Earthjustice, one of the largest and most influential environmental law firms in the world, with cases lined up against the US government for breaching its own environmental laws, or for failing to produce adequate environmental legislation. Earthjustice really goes in there to kick ass; this happens far more rarely in Britain, although Greenpeace did successfully challenge the government over its nuclear power review a couple of years ago. The methods you can use to do something similar are as follows:

Get on to the ombudsman. The local government ombudsman, for example, can ask a local authority to pay compensation if it appear to have acted improperly; the LGO's remit includes housing, transport, benefits and education. The parliamentary and health service ombudsman undertakes investigations into complaints against government departments or the NHS; if it ticks them off, they'll usually offer to sort it out, or make compensatory payments. Other areas that have ombudsmen (it's a fantastic word, isn't it? I am getting fonder of it the more often I type it. Turns out it's originally Swedish for "legal representative") include financial services, estate agents, legal services, housing and prison and probation services.

Call for a public inquiry. There's no legal framework for doing this, and it's very much at the government's discretion, so you would have to have a lot of public support. But it's potentially a useful campaign aim.

Apply for a judicial review. This is basically a way of forcing any public authority to review its decision on an issue – it's what Greenpeace used to donk the government over the head on nuclear power – and it's particularly appealing because it can be used to stop a decision before it's been implemented. The most famous example (in legal circles, anyway – this is the stuff of pillow talk for lawyers) was in 1995 and concerned the government's decision to partially fund the Pergau dam in Malaysia from its international aid budget. According to the World Development Movement, which obtained the judicial review, "government (and taxpayers') money was used to finance the project in the hope of securing future arms deals". The case brought the funding to a halt and prompted the National Audit Office to look into other aid-funded projects.

To have any chance of obtaining a review, you must first of all establish that a decision has been taken. If you are chasing, for example, a failure to take legal action against a company that has breached environmental or human rights legislation, you will need to write to the public body that should be making that decision to get a confirmation that it has decided not to act. Then you need to move fast: your application for judicial review must be lodged within three months of the decision.

The courts will then decide if they want to hear it. Do you have what is called "standing", for a start? In other words, are you sufficiently affected by the case to be allowed to bring it? (In some cases, such as the Pergau dam, the courts may consider that the issue is of sufficient national importance to waive this requirement.) The legal arguments are pretty complex: it's not just a matter of common sense and your gut feeling that the authorities have got it wrong.

Plus it's expensive, obviously, and the results are not always spectacular: there are a number of possible outcomes, the best of which are an injunction to stop the activity, an immediate overturning of the decision, or an order to undo any damage that might have been done. But further down the hierarchy is just a declaration that the decision was "unlawful", with not much follow-up. And that would be quite dull.

Try the European Commission. Recently, for example, the Clean Air In London campaign wrote to the commission with its concerns that the government was breaching the clear air directive. It emerged that the commission had already begun proceedings against the UK, but it is very willing to consider similar issues. The best way of approaching this would be to find out the name of the commissioner who deals with your area – the commissioner for industry, perhaps, or the commissioner for development and international aid – and write to them. They will be delighted to hear that someone in the UK actually knows who they are. And if you have a serious case, the government could end up in the European court.

Chapter Fourteen
Non-violence and civil disobedience

In 1888 Mohandas Gandhi, the future leader of the Indian independence movement, arrived in London to study law. This was not like his later visits, when he infuriated Churchill by attending political meetings "half naked" in a homespun sheet: at this point Gandhi was a young student, not yet 18, and he took great care with his clothes – he wore silk top hats, a Gladstonian collar and rainbow-coloured ties, and carried a silver-topped stick, in an effort to fit in a little on a continent that was then pretty much the centre of the world.

The Europe in which he found himself was at the height of its powers, both industrial and colonial. Coal, oil, electricity: the harnessing of energy in the 18th and 19th centuries had driven it ahead of the rest of the world.

Britain may have led the industrial revolution, but its neighbours were rapidly catching up, with Germany showing signs of overtaking. Big chunks of the planet – Africa, Asia, South America – had been casually divided up by the European powers so that Britain, France, Spain, Belgium and Holland all governed huge slices of the world (bad timing and political changes meant that Germany missed out on the booty), and the fruits of those empires, along with the amazing discoveries of this period, turned Europe into a bottomless toy chest of colour (synthetic colour had been discovered in 1856), sound (the phonograph was invented in 1877), light (people began to light their houses with electricity in the 1880s) and everything you could possibly imagine you wanted to buy.

Gandhi hung out at a vegetarian eating house near Fleet Street, and became a member of the Vegetarian Society of England. Through vegetarianism he met George Bernard Shaw and Annie Besant and became aware of Fabianism. He was naturally drawn to the kind of lefties and veggies that still populate the progressive movement today. But the backdrop to all this was the growing strength and confidence of Britain and Europe: richer than ever before, a consuming universe of shopping, entertainment, leisure ...

This was the world against which Gandhi saw himself and his India. It was against this voracity of appetites that he began to curb his own – literally at first, teaching himself to eat food without salt – and then in his entire way of life, living without sex with his wife, always wearing a sheet rather than the dapper outfits he had enjoyed as a student, spending a couple of hours every day spinning his own cloth as part of his drive to make India financially independent. And it was against the spiritual discordance, the arbitrary imperial governance of Europe that he formulated the campaigning tactic that sang one of the few redemptive songs of the 20th century: Satyagraha, or Love-force.

Satyagraha drew on the writings of two 19th-century oddities: the American Henry David Thoreau and the Russian Leo Tolstoy. Gandhi always said he read Thoreau's essay Civil Disobedience after he had formulated his own ideas on the subject, but it was certainly an influence on his thinking. Thoreau was the original member of the awkward squad, completely obscure in his lifetime but later a totem for Americans such as Jack Kerouac and the idea of individualism and manliness. In 1849 he refused to pay his poll tax in protest against the Mexican war and spent a night in prison. Afterwards he wrote: "Unjust laws exist: shall we be content to obey them, or shall we endeavour to amend them, and obey them until we have succeeded, or shall we transgress them at once? If the injustice is part of the necessary friction of the machine of government let it go, let it go: perchance it will run smooth ... But if it is of such a nature that it requires you to be the agent of injustice to another, then, I say, break the law ... Under a government which imprisons any injustly, the true place for a just man is ... a prison." His book would become part of American legend.

The other influence was an equally idiosyncratic but far better-known figure: Leo Tolstoy, whose books Anna Karenina and War and Peace are the novels of the human race, loved by readers and other authors then and now. They spring out of his own wrestling with the problem of how to live, a struggle he dealt with more directly in a book that particularly affected Gandhi: The Kingdom of God Is Within You, which addresses the difficulty of trying to reconcile a Christian faith with the modern world. It attacks the idea of war and asks how soldiers can be sent to kill when God and Christ specifically direct: "Thou shalt not kill." "What! All of us, Christians, not only profess to love one another, but do actually live one common life; we whose social existence beats with one common pulse – we aid one another, learn from one another, draw ever closer to one another to our mutual happiness, and find in this closeness the whole meaning of life! And tomorrow some crazy ruler will say something stupid, and another will answer in the same spirit, and then I must go expose myself to being murdered, and murder men – who have done me no harm – and more than that, whom I love. And this is not a remote contingency, but the very thing we are all preparing for, which is not only probable, but also an inevitable certainty.

"To recognise this clearly is enough to drive a man out of his senses or to make him shoot himself. And this is just what does happen, and especially often among military men. A man need only come to himself for an instant to be impelled inevitably to such an end.

"And this is the only explanation of the dreadful intensity with which men of modern times strive to stupefy themselves, with spirits, tobacco, opium, cards, reading newspapers, travelling, and all kinds of spectacles and amusements ... All men of the modern world exist in a state of continual and flagrant antagonism between their conscience and their way of life."

Tolstoy and Gandhi briefly corresponded during the last months of Tolstoy's life. Shortly before his death he wrote to the young Gandhi: "The longer I live, and especially now when I vividly feel the nearness of death, I want to tell others what I feel so particularly clearly ... namely that which is called passive resistance but which in reality is nothing else than the teaching of love, uncorrupted by false interpretations. That love ... is the highest and only law of human life." Gandhi was determined that he would find a way to make these words real: Satyagraha was to be a way of life, a political doctrine and a spiritual doctrine. As Tolstoy wrote, Gandhi had already persuaded the Indians of South Africa into mass civil disobedience – an ultimately successful protest against discrimation in Transvaal.

By January 1915 Gandhi had returned to India; straightaway he began work on the goal that would consume the rest of his life, unifying India and getting rid of the British. He pestered the British government nonstop, headed vast marches, dived with his multitudinous followers into the jails on the slightest pretext, and in 1930 led thousands of Indians to the seashore in order to defy a British tax on salt that he called "a nefarious monopoly". After walking across India for 24 days, he waded into the Arabian sea at the Gujarati village of Dandi and picked up some salt left on a rock by the waves, thus breaking the law that made it a crime to possess salt that didn't come from the British monopoly. Thousands of Indians followed suit, leading to mass arrests (100,000 by some estimates). The British army opened fire on at least one protest, but the Indians did not return force with force.

At Dharasana salt works, on a broiling day, Gandhi led hundreds of protestors against the police line that guarded the salt pans. His biographer Louis Fischer quotes the words of a journalist who was present, Webb Miller: "At a word of command, scores of native policemen rushed upon the advancing marchers and rained blows upon their heads with their steel-shod lathis. Not one of the marchers even raised an arm to fend off the blows. They went down like ninepins. From where I stood I heard the sickening whack of the clubs on unprotected skulls." When the first line had fallen, another line assembled and walked grimly forwards. "They marched steadily, with head up, without the encouragement of music or cheering or any possibility that they might escape serious injury or death. The police rushed out and methodically and mechanically beat down the second column. There was no fight, no struggle: the marchers simply walked forward till struck down." The horrible scene went on all morning, and then again the next day, and again the day after. By the end of a few days of this fearful punishment, as Fischer puts it, morally speaking "India was now free". Seventeen years later, Britain finally handed back India's independence.

In order to understand non-violence and civil disobedience as tactics, it's probably useful to separate them back out into the Tolstoyan ideal and the Thoreauvian. Both are symbolically slightly different; it is together, however, that they function best.

Thoreau's idea of civil disobedience is an apparently simple one: if a law is unjust, you must disobey it. In a dictatorship, or beneath arbitrary, discriminatory government, this makes perfect sense. In a democratic society it is a significant step forward from the idea of the right of the individual to protest against a law that he or she considers unjust. It breaks the social contract.

Tolstoy and Gandhi's ideal of nonviolence, or love-force, is a different thing: it was this idea that Richard Gregg has described so tellingly as "moral jujitsu". Gregg went out to India and met Gandhi; in an essay he wrote afterwards he describes the tactic thus: "If one man attacks another with physical violence and the victim hits back, the violent response gives the attacker a certain reassurance and moral support. It shows that the position of violence on the victim's scale of moral values is the same as that of the attacker. But suppose the assailant ... attacks a different sort of person who accepts the blows good-temperedly. The nonviolence and good will of the victim act in the same way that the lack of physical opposition by the user of physical jujitsu does, causing the attacker to lose his moral balance. He suddenly and unexpectedly loses the moral support which the usual violent resistance of most victims would render him. He plunges forward, as it were, into a new world of values."

The symbolic act here is of non-violent resistance, but you can immediately see the problem: you need something resist against. This is where the two tactics meet. If you haven't got a brutal army or a nasty police force on hand to beat you up, you're done for. The civil disobedience must provoke authority in some way, by the breaking of a law that is deemed unjust (as with all campaigns, the likelihood of success depends on the "wobbliness" of the target). So wily campaigners such as Gandhi and King used a combination of civil disobedience to create a confrontation, followed by non-violent resistance, which would give them moral superiority in that confrontation. It's cunning stuff.

King used it to particular effect in the 50s in the Montgomery bus protest, where state laws forced black people to give up their seats or get off the bus to make room for whites. The campaign is usually referred to as the Montgomery Bus Boycott, but King had great reservations about the idea of a boycott as a policy. He agonised: "Were we following an ethical course of action? Is the boycott method basically un-Christian? Isn't it a negative approach to the solution of a problem?

"As I thought further I came to see that what we were really doing was withdrawing our cooperation from an evil system, rather than merely withdrawing our support from the bus company ... From this moment on I conceived of our movement as an act of massive non-cooperation. From then on I rarely used the word 'boycott'." The Montgomery campaign carried on with unflinching discipline for another year, King was arrested, the city tried numerous methods of penalising him and the protestors and was about to put an injunction on the well-organised car pool that had sustained the protest when a message came that the US supreme court had declared that the local laws that upheld segregation were unconstitutional.

In this case local laws were illegal within the context of national laws. A couple of years later, when the civil rights campaign had grown and begun to intermingle with the anti-Vietnam campaign, civil disobedience was used far less effectively. By then the young students who were organising sit-ins and die-ins all over the country used to grumble about the way that King took credit for the movement, but the fact is that, like Gandhi, he was a brilliant tactician who saw clearly where victories could be won and momentum gained for the campaign, and tried to avoid situations where demoralising defeat would be the result.

But in 1963 he was assassinated. The students who were protesting against the Vietnam war had seen his tactics in action in the search of civil rights for African Americans, and believed they could be straightforwardly transferred to this particular battle; King was not there to disabuse them. Numerous acts of mass civil disobedience occurred, such as the protests at the Pentagon where thousands, including Noam Chomsky and Norman Mailer, staged sit-down protests and refused to be moved, forcing the federal marshals who were policing the march to arrest them. The massive anti-war movement that sprang up inspired a US government worker to a further, high-ranking act of civil disobedience: Daniel Ellsberg's leak of a 7,000-page top-secret report into American involvement in Vietnam known as the Pentagon Papers.

Ellsberg's decision to betray his government arose from his moral certainty that this war, this course of action, was wrong, and this certainty hardened as he saw young protestors fighting so desperately against it. After one political meeting of the War Resisters League where the campaigners discussed non-violence and agreed that going to jail would have to be the next step, Ellsberg found his way to a toilet and began to cry, unable to stop himself for an hour. "We are eating our young, I thought again, sitting on the floor of the men's room … On both sides of the barricades we are using them, using them up, 'wasting' them. This is what my country has come to. We have come to this. The best thing that the best young men of our country can do with their lives is to go to prison." However, even his leaking of the Pentagon Papers did not embarrass the US government into withdrawing from Vietnam.

The problem is that the anti-war campaign, as we have seen elsewhere, is a very special case. Governments will back down in areas that are not central to their policy, but on war they are usually intransigent. The 1968 anti-Vietnam protests could not stop the killing, and it was not until 1974 that Congress finally passed an act that would take Americans out of the war. Where King was targeting situations that were contrary to the spirit of American law, and so rectifiable, the anti-war demonstrators were asking for a complete paradigm shift. War? Wrong?

In his book Secrets: A Memoir of Vietnam and the Pentagon Papers, Ellsberg includes tapes of Nixon's discussions with Kissinger that reveal his attitude to war. The president thumped a map on the table as he tried to explain to his staff how things were: "Vietnam, here's those little cocksuckers right in there, here they are. [Thump.] Here's the United States. [Thump.] Here's western Europe, that cocky little place that's caused so much devastation ... Here's the Soviet Union [thump], here's the [thump] Mid-East ... Here's the [thump] silly Africans ... And [thump] the not-quite-so-silly Latin Americans. Here we are. They're taking on the United States. Now, goddammit, we're gonna do it. We're going to cream them ... I should have done it long ago, I just didn't follow my instincts ... I'll see that United States does not lose. I'm putting it quite bluntly. I'll be quite precise. South Vietnam may lose. But the United States cannot lose. Which means, basically, I have made the decision. Whatever happens to South Vietnam, we are going to cream North Vietnam ... For once, we've got to use the maximum power of this country ... against this shit-ass little country: to win the war." One can imagine similar recordings one day emerging of conversations in the White House ahead of the Iraq war. Ellsberg adds: "In a later exchange Nixon observed to Kissinger: 'The only place where you and I disagree ... is with regard to the bombing. You're so goddamned concerned about the civilians and I don't give a damn. I don't care.' Kissinger responded: 'I'm concerned about the civilians because I don't want the world to be mobilised against you as a butcher.'"

Why I fight

Caroline Harvey
Anti-wind turbine activist with the Two Moors Campaign

It was all rather out of the blue: one of our neighbours knocked on the door and told us that they were applying to build a wind turbine on their land. They'd wanted to tell us before, but the developers had said not to mention it. My first reaction was just, "Right, OK." And then they told us it was going to be 100 metres tall.

We've lived in this part of the world for 10 years: our farm is in a very rural part of North Devon and we like the quietness, it's what we looked for. There are nine giant wind turbines proposed opposite the entrance to our farm, all 103m high and on ground 50m metres higher than we are. The wind turbine would be right in front of us, 730 metres away; there would be the noise, the moving of the blades, and they're even talking about lighting it at night to warn low-flying aircraft. I was absolutely gutted – for the first three months I kept bursting into tears thinking about it. I tried to think, "Well, at least it's doing some good." But then I started to look into it, and that just upset me even more.

Most energy firms are only putting wind turbines up because the government is subsidising them so heavily. Everyone loves them because they're like an advertisement – they say "We're doing something", when actually we should be putting the money into something far more useful. The energy companies are exagerating the amount of power that their turbines will produce, and with wind power you have to allow for the fact that it's so unpredictable, whereas with tidal power the tide always goes out and it always comes in. But because wind power looks so much more impressive, the government is pouring money into it. The figures for the electricity the turbines produce is hugely over-optimistic, and often don't take into account the fact that the wind just doesn't blow 24 hours a day.

We've been fighting against the turbine for more than two years, and there are now four more sites putting in applications. It's damaged the community: I know that the children of the families who are applying for permission have had some trouble at school, and I'm really sad that we've found ourselves in this position. But I've met a whole range of people I would never have spoken to. If the turbines go up we'll just have to sit here and see how things go.

Against that backdrop, against a surging America, financially and politically full of confidence, not inclined to admit mistakes, the anti-war protestors would not win. It's a sad defeat, one of the great scars in the history of protest. Some of those protestors moved on to violence. Others, a huge number, certainly lost all belief in democratic protest.

But maybe they should have more faith. Non-violent civil resistance is attracting a lot of attention these days. A couple of years ago an organisation called Freedom House brought out a report called How Freedom Is Won: From Civic Resistance to Durable Democracy. The study looked at 67 countries that had made or attempted to make a transition from being "not free" or "partially free" to "free", measuring the strength of civil society at the time and the amount of violence offered by both protestors and the state. The conclusion it reached was extremely interesting: "The presence of strong and cohesive non-violent civic coalitions is the most important of the factors examined in contributing to freedom." Of the 35 countries to have achieved "free" status, 32 had a significant civic resistance component.

Adam Roberts, senior research fellow at the Centre for International Studies in Oxford, is in the process of editing a study, Civil Resistance and Power Politics, on this subject. He points, in particular, to the events in eastern Europe in 1989–91 as a series of countries peacefully stepped away from Communist Party rule. "That is one example where civil resistance was effective," he says. He is dubious, however, about suggestions that western governments should fund civil movements as part of their foreign policy. "Independence from foreign finance is quite important, otherwise it sometimes happens that groups start to be regarded with some suspicion." He also makes the point that civil resistance is not an answer to every situation, and that the context in which the resistance takes place is all-important: "Against a really thuggish state, as, for example in Burma the resistance had limited effectiveness. Although in that case the Burmese government is now so discredited that the situation may begin to shift at last." Even if it doesn't move the earth tomorrow, it is deeply pleasing to think that Gandhi's "love-force" is now being studied in the tranquil rooms of Oxford University.

So how might you use it now? Firstly – this is kind of obvious but worth stating anyway – it's useless against corporations, because it specifically expresses discontent with the government, which sets the legal structure within which we operate. So the issues to which it might apply are things such as privacy laws, the Iraq war (where the government was perceived by many to have acted illegally), and other government policies that you believe to be wrong. You can't do civil disobedience against McDonald's.

There are apparent exceptions to this, such as the case of the Skye Bridge protest, in which users of a new privately run link between the Isle of Skye and the mainland of Scotland refused to pay unexpectedly high tolls. (Fuelling their resistance was the fact that the bridges of other nearby islands were public roads and therefore free.) But while this may originally have looked like a straightforward strike against a private company, after numerous prosecutions for non-payment, and a continuing hubbub of anger, it came to be seen as a civil rights issue that only government could resolve. In 2004 the Scottish government stepped in, bought the bridge, and declared it toll-free from here on in. The private company had, of course, made a handsome profit on the deal.

Secondly, doh, it's illegal: you are breaking a law. One of the greatest challenges of this particular tactic is to find a way of practising civil disobedience that is acceptable to a large proportion of the general population, otherwise you will be perceived as a simple criminal. The mass non-payment of Margaret Thatcher's hugely unpopular poll tax, for example, was seen by many people, even those not doing it, as "only right". The tax, after all, was manifestly unjust.

And campaigners quickly spotted the potential of the clause in the Serious Organised Crime and Police Act 2005 that forbade protest in Parliament Square: like the discrimination against black bus passengers in Montgomery, it contravened what the population perceived as the essential spirit of the law, the social contract. When protestors fell foul of the clause, or found a way round it – as with with Milan Rai and Maya Evans' arrest for reading the names of dead soldiers on the Cenotaph, or the weekly picnics on Parliament Square – they did so with majority support: the right to protest on any bit of public land you like is central to Britain's idea of itself. I went along to one anti-war camp in Parliament Square in summer 2007 where rumours were circulating that the clause was about to be dropped; the police weren't even bothering to arrest anyone, and it was bringing the whole camp down a bit. They'd come to be arrested, even done a workshop on the best way of resisting arrest the night before, and now the police were just ignoring them. In a funny way it was a mirror image of civil resistance.

But people have found other ways of committing civil disobedience in relation to Iraq – from refusing to serve in the army, to refusing to pay the portion of tax that would go to the Ministry of Defence, like the Peace Tax Seven, who are currently taking their case to the European Court of Justice. Robin Brookes, one of the seven, is a Quaker, and three years ago he decided that he just could not bear to support the Iraq war with his taxes any longer: it was against his religion. So he calculated what percentage of his tax went to the Ministry of Defence, and then he paid the rest and sent a letter to the tax office saying that he had put this portion into a bank account and would be happy to put it toward another branch of the government – but he did not want it to be spent on war. He has done this, along with six other people, every year since: one year he handed over the money to the bailiffs in the end when they came, another he was arrested, and now, with the help of Keir Starmer, the lawyer who helped to advise Helen Steel and Dave Morris in the McLibel case, he is taking his case to Europe.

(In fact, it's worth noting that the Iraq war has been so incredibly unpopular and felt to be so illegitimate itself by the general population that even acts that would normally be considered beyond the pale, such as the Fairford Two's attempt to sabotage US bombers, are deemed acceptable by a jury. Phil Pritchard and Toby Olditch's defence was that they were trying to prevent a greater crime, the murder of innocent Iraqi civilians. They were acquitted of criminal damage – despite expecting a five-year sentence – in May 2007.)

Adam Roberts remarked to me how often civil resistance breaks out in order to assert a people's perceived democratic rights: in Ukraine, for example, when the election was perceived to have been conducted illegally. Civil disobedience, or Satyagraha, or Love-force, or passive resistance – whatever name you choose for it – has proven to be one of the most powerful and eloquent tools we can use to express our sense of injustice, or to make a call for equality. It's extremely specialised, but in the hands of the right person, standing in the right place, like Archimedes' lever it can move the world.

Chapter Fifteen
Direct action

These days direct action is used in the name of all sorts of causes. Anarchists travel to Palestine and go on daylight raids to cut holes in the wire fence that Israeli soldiers patrol. Tree-sitters try to hold off the chainsaws in Dalkeith Country Park. Members of the Ontario Coalition Against Poverty invade employment offices with megaphones, demanding improved welfare rates. The Norwich branch of Rising Tide blockades an Esso petrol station. Katuah Earth First! blocks the road to a mine that threatens the destruction of Zeb Mountain. Bored? Nothing to do? Why not chain yourself to the nearest railing?

When the Women's Institute sends its members into supermarkets to kick up a stink about excessive packaging, you know direct action has hit the mainstream. It has been growing in popularity for about 40 years now, ever since the death of Martin Luther King and the frustration of the campaign against the Vietnam war. Direct action has always existed, obviously – in some senses any kind of action is direct action – but I'd trace the idea, the form, of direct action that we have today back to the confrontations between anti-war protestors and the authorities in the late 60s. The anti-war movement had been educated by Martin Luther King in non-violence, and looked to Gandhi for inspiration, but as the violence escalated, and particularly after the landmark Pentagon demonstration in 1967 where marshals waded into a sit-in with their batons, the idea of being passively cracked over the head began to seem less and less attractive. An anti-conscription demo in Oakland gave the campaigners the clue to their next move: the activist Marvin Garson described in the Village Voice the way that, rather than sit still and be beaten up or dragged away, the demonstrators retreated from the police, splitting like amoebae, taking control of traffic intersections in an ever-widening circle. With hardly any arrests or injuries, they managed to keep the army's induction centre closed for three hours. Garson concluded: "Everyone in Berkeley [one of the universities at the centre of the antiwar protests] today knows that we'll never sit down again." A fellow anti-war activist, Martin Jezer, considered that "in a sense [the] confrontation at the Pentagon was a last sit-down for us ... Why the sit-down? Why the passivity? Why did we so easily get ourselves into the position where beatings were inevitable? Why couldn't we, for once, have let our imaginations and creativity run wild, trust ourselves, and do something different? American pacifists have performed a disservice to the non-violent movement in America by narrowly defining non-violence in terms of Gandhi's Indian experience. Satyagrahis we are not. Americans have neither the patience nor the discipline to feel comfortable in such a bag. Moreover, the concern with Gandhian non-violence ignores some of the most positive characteristics of the American people ... I am talking of spontaneity and creativity."

Direct activists are an entirely different constituency from Gandhi's Satyagrahis. Physical protest, until this moment, had been undertaken solely by the affected themselves, on their own behalf – the suffragettes asking for the vote, the Indians looking for independence, the African-Americans demanding their civil rights. But here we are in the 60s with some of the world's most privileged people raising Cain on behalf of some of its poorest and most helpless. When Gandhi or King practised civil disobedience, they were revolting against a system that they had played no part in creating but that had them at its mercy. (King said that a law could be described as unjust "if it is inflicted on a minority that, as a result of being denied the right to vote, had no part in enacting or devising the law".) The direct activists are protesting on behalf of others, whether it's the Vietnamese, or whales, or South Africans suffering under apartheid.

They are not excluded, in democratic terms, from the system. They simply find it wanting: they object to a system that would pursue a war, or a racial or environmental policy that they consider wrong. Their demands are not for more anything – more rights, more votes, more wages. They are for something "different". Direct action – putting your body in the way – seems entirely appropriate as a way of trying to derail this system with which they disagree so fervently.

Who are these protestors? Are they work-shy? Bonkers? Stupid idealists? Are they spoiled kids with nothing better to do, who are just dissatisfied with the status quo and get a bit of an adrenaline rush from fighting police? Well, there's certainly an element of that. Activists themselves acknowledge the problem of "ego-activism", and you'll hear many discussions about the machismo that often pulls movements apart. I very much enjoyed the touching and faintly ridiculous account that Robert Hunter gives of the very earliest days of Greenpeace: it all seems to have been one long tripped out adventure. Thanks to, as Hunter puts it, "an extraordinarily high percentage of beautiful, intelligent, liberated, radiant, positive females, most of them single", divorce rates in the group soared, and "the light of love hovered like a nimbus over all our gatherings, infusing the atmosphere with tremendous surges of primal energy". As they set off with their little inflatable boats to find the huge whaling ships for confrontations that were astonishingly brave – and, until recently, extremely effective, in limiting the activities of whalers – Hunter, who had run most of this particular journey by meditation and the I Ching, reflected: "It seemed to me that we were like a seagoing gang of ecological bikers, bikers who had adopted the Satyagraha philosophy of Mahatma Gandhi, but who rode high-powered roaring machines across the waves and whose collective aggressive energy was more in tune at times with the mood of pillagers descending on a helpless village than 1960s hippies coming to tuck flowers into the rifles of national guardsmen."

At the very same time as the ecological bikers were rolling, however, a more straightforward campaign was being waged in the UK. There had been protests against apartheid for some years by that point, but in 1969 young British campaigners took exception to a national tour by the South African rugby team, with the cricket team due to follow soon afterwards. They began the Stop The Seventy campaign, buying tickets for the rugby matches and chucking themselves on to the pitches, trying to handcuff themselves to the goalposts and generally getting in the way, often at risk of being beaten up by irate fans who did not want to see their games interrupted.

Peter Hain, now a Labour MP, was one of the main organisers. "Non-violent direct action," he told me, "was a good way of mobilising people without getting into all the boring wrangles over constitutions and meetingitis that so many campaign groups get stuck in. Did it have any impact beyond getting the rugby tour cancelled? Well, the cricket tour was also cancelled. And Nelson Mandela told me it had a real impact on him. There was a complete news blackout at Robben Island, of course, but the warders were such sports fanatics that they just couldn't keep quiet about it. His point was that because South Africans were so shunned by the rest of the world, sports was one of the few places where they could take their place in the public arena and it gave them a huge psychological boost. So it was a huge blow for them. But of course it was many years before apartheid came apart, and that was due to many forces coming to play." (Hain also mentioned, to my astonishment, that Gordon Brown was down as one of their organisers in Edinburgh. Does the Daily Mail know about this?)

So direct action is not just about hippy dreams. It is also a solid, extremely effective tactic that can be used by any campaigner, even if he or she is seeking something slightly less complex then international peace and harmony. The two campaigns, through simultaneous, were very different: although Greenpeace's ostensible aim was an environmental one, its campaign was also on behalf of its members and a kind of deep dissatisfaction with the modern world, a restless search for a new spiritual truth, a new way of being. The same cannot be said of the wholly pragmatic Stop The Seventy campaign, which had a stated aim – to stop the sports tours – and was dissolved as an organisation as soon as this aim had been fulfilled. Direct action, when applied to a situation like this, continues to be astonishingly effective. But the larger spiritual quest? This is a problem with which the pacifists, environmentalists, anti-capitalists and anarchists (who may or may not be the same people) continue to wrestle.

Over the past couple of decades of often tumultuous use, direct action has managed some fantastic victories, particularly on environmental issues. The 70s were nonstop, on everything from homelessness (where Ron Bailey, who we met in the chapter on lobbying, managed to force radical improvements in temporary accommodation) to nuclear weapons. British activism in the 80s mostly centred on political issues around the miners' strike and class war, but the States saw the birth of the Earth First! movement, which promoted direct action on behalf of the planet. In the early 90s Jason Torrance and Jake Bowers set up a UK branch of Earth First! and it took off like a rocket: they began with protests at Liverpool docks over the importation of illegally logged tropical hardwoods, but then really found their feet with the campaign to prevent Twyford Down being sliced through for the M3 motorway. The 90s anti-road campaign began there and continued at the site for the proposed extension of the M11, and then the Newbury bypass, accompanied by a huge growth of green campaigning muscle as other environmental groups either came on board (Friends of the Earth, for example, was very late to join in but came around to direct action during Newbury, after which it was extremely supportive) or were formed, such at This Land Is Ours, fighting to reclaim the land for the people. Meanwhile in the cities, Reclaim The Streets was staging huge, wonderful street parties, which eventually became one of the trademarks of a brand new global movement. By the end of the 90s the environmental direct action movement had encouraged the Tories to call a halt to the roads programme, and brought the issue of genetically modified foods into the public eye.

The noughties have seen campaigns against the over-packaging of food, which has jolted supermarkets into acknowledging the need for change, and the growth in aviation, which has kept airlines and their emissions in the headlines. In Wales and the west of Ireland, new gas pipelines have been the subject of unwanted attention. Direct action, done well, is probably one of the best ways of raising awareness and even getting a final concession.

Many of these actions have involved breaking the law: criminal damage, harassment, obstructing the highway, aggravated trespass … But direct action does not have to be illegal: it simply involves putting yourself on the line. You could, in WI style, bring back handfuls of packaging to your local supermarket – this will not land you in a police cell. Even entering an office or a shop to stage a sit-in – as long as you do it peacefully without forcing entry – is not a criminal offence because trespass is a civil matter. This means that although the owners of the shop or office may be entitled to sue you for loss of earnings or damage (I have not come across any cases of this actually occurring) you are not actually acting illegally.

If you want to keep out of court, the two main areas to be aware of are trespass law (covered at length towards the end of this chapter) and obstructing the highway (which makes all blockading, from D-locking yourself to a gate, through concreting yourselves together across a road, to using vehicles to block access, illegal). But you also need to consider your manner: if your behaviour can be construed in any way as threatening or distressing, you can be prosecuted under the Criminal Justice Act 1994. The Protection from Harassment Act 1997, meanwhile, allows organisations to seek injunctions against people whose actions amount to "harassment", which seems to include causing distress to employees, or intimidation or obstruction. Obviously this is incredibly broad and open to misuse: I've heard of one case where a protestor was done for talking to a digger operator and stopping him getting on with his work.

However, it's important to remember that however well-behaved you are, the police may still arrest you. The shocking truth is that you do not have to be doing anything illegal in order to be arrested. If you are "making a nuisance of yourself", it is entirely possible that the police will just haul you off and, if so inclined, think of a charge later.

Still, you may well feel the risk is worth running. Direct action is cheap, and quick and easy to organise, so small groups with small resources can just get on with it – you only need a handful of people with nerves of steel to stage an occupation of your local town hall. It's exhilarating: it charges up the "insurrectionary imagination" in a way that few other forms of protest ever can, so once you've steeled yourself to tear all the wrappers off your vegetables at the Marks & Spencer checkout and lived to tell the tale, you'll find yourself twitching to do it again, just for the high.

Ctrl.Alt.Shift: October 19 2009

Direct action must be full of moments when you think "what on earth am I doing?" I had one of those last weekend. I went along to follow the Climate Camp protestors who were targeting Ratcliffe on Soar power station, and, after an afternoon full of incident, during which both a protestor and a police officer collapsed and had to be stretchered away from the scene, there was a meeting in the woods about what to do next.

It was decided that protestors would try one more time to get into the plant; half the group would go one way and create a diversion, while the other half would sneak round to the north west point where the fences were weakest and try to get in. I followed my journalistic instinct (also my natural instinct unfortunately) to go where there was most likely to be trouble, and followed the second group.

And there began the most ridiculous, hilarious wander through the woods of my life. The idea was to sneak around under cover, and a couple of the activists had clearly already spent plenty of time getting to know the area. They led us up across a field (past two policemen on motorbikes, so the cover was blown straight away), into a small copse, and then along a line of woodland up above the northern line of the power station perimeter. Halfway along another policeman on a motorbike peered into the woodland and we all lay down on our stomachs and then carried on – crawling under brambles, climbing over strands of barbed wire.

After what felt like half an hour, when darkness was falling, I had lost all sense of direction and was just longing to be at home with my children, watching The X Factor. At this point someone sent a whisper back that we were nearly there. My phone vibrated in my pocket: it was an editor wanting to know what was going on. I sat down in a puddle of mud in the dark middle of the bush, as the bottoms of activists disappeared like rabbits into a tiny hole in the undergrowth in front of me, and tried to describe the scene. "Stay safe!" he said, audibly sipping from a cup of tea down the other end of the phone. I have never wanted a cup of tea so much in my life.

When I got through the hole myself, it was to find a police spotlight trained upon us all. At this point an overwhelming sense of "that's enough" swept over me. I no longer cared about arrests. I no longer cared about watching people getting into the plant. All I could think about was getting into my car, finding a service station and having some dinner. By now it really was dark, and I was starving, so I turned back and set off along the path (why hadn't we just taken the path?) that runs around the perimeter. A black-hooded anarchist fell in beside me, and as we sauntered through the woods and past the police still stationed beneath spotlights by the fence, we had an amiable conversation about the roots of the Zapatista struggle. One police van honked, and I wondered if we should wave, and then decided it was politer to just pretend they weren't there.

Direct action, man. If your life is sadly lacking the surreal, this is definitely the place to be.

And it can be massively embarrassing for the company involved, or for the government, and, as we've seen, shame is one of the most potent weapons a protestor has. Governments do not want to be exposed for breaking promises on homelessness, or international aid – they will lose votes. Companies do not want to be exposed for using child labour or committing crimes against the environment – they will lose customers. Many activists report that once you have targeted a company, it is likely to give way more quickly next time. The more hardcore versions of direct action, such as blockading or sabotage, can also cause delays and huge financial costs for big projects like road building; that is anathema to companies and has led to them pulling out of projects in the past.

But what do I mean by "hardcore"? Well, the thing about direct action is that it is not one specific tactic but rather a spectrum of them. And people take up very definite positions on that spectrum, the believers in non-violence at one end and at the other the freedom fighters/terrorists. Yup, that's right. If you set up a guerrilla group in, say, the Caledonian forests of the Scottish Highlands (there's not much of them left but you've still got 180 square kilometres to run around in), read Che Guevara's Guerrilla Warfare, do a lot of marching and target practice and then return to civilisation to take on the … I dunno, whoever your target might be, you could also be considered a direct activist. A lot of activists will hate you for betraying the ethos of the movement. But frankly, that's probably going to be the least of your worries.

Somewhere between these two positions is where most believers in direct action stand, and you can place yourself wherever you want. You may be committed to direct action but not want to put yourself at risk of physical harm or arrest; in that case you will want to stay in the legal zone (where, for someone with imagination, there are still plenty of possibilities). You may be prepared to risk arrest and harm to yourself, in which case bring on the invasions, sit-ins, blockades and lock-ons. This is where the common perception of direct action lies: it's the sort of stuff that went on in the 90s over the Newbury bypass. In the next stage you may be prepared to cause damage to someone else's property, either through sabotage or with a baseball bat: this position takes you into the quasi-violent end of things. The GM crops protests that took place up and down the country in the late 90s fell into this category. You may be prepared to suffer or even die for your cause, like the IRA man Bobby Sands, who died after a prolonged hunger strike in Maze prison in 1981, or Norman Morrison, who set himself on fire and burned to death outside the Pentagon in protest against the Vietnam war in 1965.

The Guardian: September 16 2008

To begin a hunger strike seems to me a step so drastic, so serious, that it puts a chill in my veins. Maura Harrington, however, is completely resolute, and at the same time still capable of making jokes. If I wasn't talking to her over a phone I'd perhaps want to shake her.

Her hunger strike, which began last Tuesday and was still carrying on last night, is another chapter in the ongoing battle between the local residents of Rossport in County Mayo, Ireland and the multinational oil company Shell. For eight years now the community has been fighting against plans to build a pipeline from an offshore gas extraction outfit through or near Rossport and on to an onshore refinery.

The local people have become bitterly divided, the Rossport Five have famously served time in jail, a protest camp has taken root near the village, fishermen are out in their boats trying to face down Shell's machinery and now Harrington has gone on hunger strike out of sheer fury and desperation. As local campaigner Terence Conway says, "The days before we were fighting this seem like childhood memories now. It just goes on, day after day after day."

The months of the summer have seen the turmoil of this community worsen as Shell begins finally to lay the bitterly resented offshore pipeline, despite the fact the onshore route is still in dispute.

The situation is this: Shell now have permission to lay their offshore pipeline through the waters of Broadhaven Bay, on which the village of Rossport sits, to the land. Shell's ship, the Solitaire, is moving into position to do this.

Harrington, a former headmistress, has been opposed to the onshore pipeline from the start, and believes Shell should build an offshore refinery. She gave notice to the commander of Shell's Solitaire boat that if it came into the bay she would begin her strike and carry on till the ship went away.

How is she feeling? "Alright, it's early days still." She's eating nothing, and only drinking water, and given her smallness – she only weights 42kg (6st 9lb) already – she can't have many reserves. The hunger strike is something she's been contemplating for months now, but the decision was finally made when she heard that the Solitaire was on its way. It sprang out of her despair, she says, over the actions not just of Shell but of the local authorities, the Garda, and the government.

"What kind of country are we living in?" she says. "This part of the world was such a beautiful place, and it is painful, physically and emotionally, to see what has happened here with the construction work. So I have put my life and death into the hands of the Solitaire."

Conway is deeply worried: he says that after seven days the effect is beginning to show. "I've never met the captain of the Solitaire, I don't know the man, but I hope he will help us resolve this somehow."

The latest development is damage to the Solitaire: Shell have already announced they will be removing it for repairs. At the moment Harrington does not plan to stop: she says she trusts Shell "about as far as I can throw the Solitaire". But even if she does stop, she will certainly start again when the boat returns. Is this courageousness or madness?

Or you may be prepared to cause actual bodily harm. Ah yes, the violence that the media is always waiting for …

Is violence ever a justifiable tactic? This question has been chewed over so often by campaign groups. It's a question that immediately provokes three more, irritatingly, and we'll have to look at them one by one. Firstly, what do you mean by violence? Secondly, what is your personal position on the use of violence? And thirdly, does violence work?

The first question – what do you mean by violence? – refers to the fact that violence, although one of the biggest, most emotive words in the language, is actually a bit of a chimera. In his thought-provoking book How Nonviolence Protects the State, the anarchist Peter Gelderloos describes a workshop he gave: "I conducted a little exercise to demonstrate how vague this idea of violence really is. I asked the participants, who included supporters of non-violence and supporters of a diversity of tactics, to stand up and, as I slowly read a list of various actions, to walk to one spot if they considered the action violent, and to another if they considered the action non-violent. The actions included such things as buying clothes made in a sweatshop, eating meat, a wolf eating a deer, killing someone who is about to detonate a bomb in a crowd, and so on. Almost never was there perfect agreement among the participants." He describes violence as "a concept so blurry that no two people can really agree on what it means".

Why I fight

Dave Currey
Undercover environmental investigator

You can make as much money out of wildlife trafficking as you can from smuggling cocaine, but the penalties are much much lighter because no one takes it as seriously. Basically, as undercover investigators, we at the Environmental Investigation Agency deal with a bunch of crooks, and sometimes they're great fun, and you find yourself having dinner with them. But one thing they never understand about us, and that we understand very well about them and that gives us an advantage over them, is that we're not doing it for money. And they are doing whatever they're doing – smuggling ivory, illegal logging, poaching tigers – for money.

I met Allan Thornton (who's now chairman of EIA's American office) on the Greenpeace ship Rainbow Warrior in 1979. I was incredibly seasick the whole time, and used to get up and be sick twice, and then start the day. But somehow he still persuaded me and Jenny Lonsdale on to another boat up to Norway four years later, where we were the first to tackle Norwegian whaling. We managed to get loads of information about the hunt, we spoke to the buyers and got into the factories and realised when we got back to Britain that there was no one around to really produce that sort of info. So a year later we set up the Environmental Investigation Agency.

Over the years since then I've spent lengthy periods undercover for one reason or another. It can get a bit hairy, but you get a feeling about when to get out, when your cover is starting to get thin. At a few points, during the two years I spent undercover investigating the ivory trade, I narrowly missed meeting people who I'd met earlier under a different identity. But I think we played an important part in achieving the international ban on ivory trading. We're here to embarrass and to encourage governments into action with the information they should have come up with, but haven't. And along the way, I have to say, there are quite a few laughs as well.

Most of us probably think of violence as bodily harm – something done to another person. But in protest terms it's usually conceived of by legal bodies as including damage to property, which makes it a bit more all-inclusive. In 2002 the FBI defined eco-terrorism as "the use or threatened use of violence of a criminal nature against innocent victims or property by an environmentally oriented, sub-national group for environmental-political reasons, or aimed at an audience beyond the target, often of a symbolic nature". One environmental activist said to me: "'Violence' is often used by the press, politicians and other commentators to describe action that damages property. Many, including me, would contest that such action is 'violent'. I have never come across anyone who would condone violence towards people, as opposed to damage to inanimate property. Any action I've come across is under the banner of peaceful direct action – it might be illegal, it might cost the target money, but it is peaceful and would not risk injury of people. This kind of action does sometimes get labelled as a form of terrorism, which I would say is a deeply inaccurate and unethical use of that word."

So, first of all, define your terms.

Second question: where do you yourself stand on all this? It is down to every individual to make their own choices about their willingness to commit violence, whether it be against property or people. It's interesting how often our positions are not as clear as we would imagine, even to ourselves. And there is a difference, remember, between what you perceive to be acceptable and what is socially perceived as acceptable. Self-defence, or defence of your family (one of the oddest moments after having my first son was realising that I was capable of attacking and even killing anyone who tried to hurt him: it was the first time I'd really been aware of any violent streak in myself, and it was weird – both unnerving and empowering at the same time), or defence of the country against enemies are usually seen as acceptable kinds of violence; after that things start to get more complicated. The only legitimate violence (after self-defence) is monopolised by the state: this is the social contract as prescribed by Hobbes, in which, to avoid living in a world "warre of every man against every man" we all surrender our rights and our freedom to fight to one higher authority. Deliberate violence against another person, therefore, breaks the social contract.

So you will not find a social justification for violence. You are on your own with this.

And so we arrive at question three: is violence effective? I had assumed lazily that violence didn't really work, that it alienated support and forced the authorities into an entrenched position where they might not dare to make concessions for fear of appearing weak. But I was set straight by a history professor who said crisply: "Violence works. It's politically correct nonsense to suggest that it doesn't." And funnily enough, on page 403 of the Handbook of Policing, a comprehensive overview of policing in the UK, it says of protest: "Violence works! [William] Gamson reviewed a large array of American social movements and found that those which made recourse to violence succeeded more often than those that did not."

I looked up William Gamson: in 1990 he reviewed 53 American social movements and found that those that used violence (which he defined as "deliberate physical injury to property or persons"), really did show a significantly higher rate of success. Of the 53 movements, eight used violence themselves (unions fighting the police, anti-communists fighting communists, protectionist farmers making their point through arson), seven were the targets of violence (non-violent civil rights campaigners visiting the American south, etc) and 36 movements did not involve violence. The first group, the violent lot, had a 73 per cent success rate in gaining new advantages for themselves; the second, the recipients of violence, had no success at all; and the third managed a 52 per cent success rate. And when the groups that aimed to displace their antagonists altogether, rather than just win some concessions, were taken out of the calculation, the violent group did even better, achieving a 100 per cent success rate in gaining new advantages, while the third group rose to 72 per cent. So it looks good for violence, doesn't it? As Gamson puts it, violence "is commonly believed to be self-defeating. Evaluating the validity of this belief is made elusive by a tendency that we all have, social scientists and laymen alike, to allow our moral judgments to influence our strategic judgments and vice versa."

This is just one study, however. In reality, even when a campaign involving violence is victorious, it's hard to know whether it was the violence that won the day. Take the suffragettes – to what extent can we credit the militant tactics employed in the early 20th century with finally winning the vote for women? The suffragette campaign followed the usual arc: it started back in the 16th century with radicals such as Mary Wollstonecraft, speaking the unspeakable in her book A Vindication of the Rights of Woman (1792). A movement began to grow of like-minded folk: wonderful women such as Josephine Butler, Elizabeth Garrett Anderson and Millicent Fawcett used lobbying and petitions and letter-writing campaigns to move things forwards. But progress was so achingly slow. And so, as it began to look as if peaceful means would get the cause nowhere, one group turned to violence – and within a decade women had the vote.

Was it the violent tactics that finally won? The lengths the suffragettes went to are shocking, even now: tying themselves to the gates of the House of Commons, window-breaking, arson, even suicide, as well as the hunger strikes in prison and the subsequent force-feeding, accounts of which are dizzyingly painful to read. It's easy to understand why the campaigners felt forced to take this position: the intransigence of the British government on this issue, in the face of tremendous marches and lobbying, is breathtaking. But if anything, the violence increased that intransigence and gave the government an excuse to continue refusing, on the grounds that it would not bend to militancy. You can argue that it was the first world war that finally untied the issue, not militant tactics at all. But you can also argue that the militant tactics made the issue one of such urgency and national importance that the British government was forced to give way the moment it was expedient to do so – when it could look as if it was not giving in to terrorism. You can, in short, argue till the cows come home.

And you can have similar arguments about non-violent campaigns such as those led by Mahatma Gandhi and Martin Luther King, because after all weren't those campaigns mounted against a background of rising violence and threatened revolution? What was it that persuaded governments to give in to the demands of Gandhi and King: their non-violence, or fear of the violence that might erupt if their demands were refused? The problem is that the moment when a campaign is won is often sudden and unexpected: something gives somewhere, a lever is pulled abruptly, and the decision is taken. It's impossible to know, much of the time, what actually caused the victory. But, however you want to look at it, there's no doubt that violence or threatened violence is often one, if not the sole, factor in winning a campaign.

As a side note, violence is fantastically successful at getting an issue into the public eye. As publicity stunts go, you can't fault it – you'll get the front page every time. Bombing campaigns, suicide bombings – these are the extreme end of violent campaigning, and they get attention, they focus people's minds on issues such as Iraq. Do they help resolve it, though? Once again, it's impossible to pick the situation apart to reveal the truth: the conclusion you reach is almost inevitably influenced by your own moral position, as Gamson pointed out.

So, with all this in mind, is violence ever justifiable as a tactic? After all, there are plenty of options that don't involve hurting someone or putting a life at risk. And look again at Gamson's figures: those who did not use violence still managed a 52 and 72 per cent success rate; that's not bad, is it? Violence, you must remember, is more than just a tactic: it has a mind of its own, it gets out of control, it twists round and destroys any notion of justice or fairness. A Palestinian boy throws a stone at an Israeli soldier; what are the consequences of that act? How many times will it be amplified before a gunman enters a school full of children, before the armies set up their rockets, before a suicide bomber walks into the marketplace?

When you choose force as the way to make your point, you leave yourself open to having force used against you. And after that the winner is just the person with the biggest muscles, the most powerful gun, the best-constructed bomb. Violence has a scale and a hierarchy all its own. One of the activists involved in the anti-capitalist movement told me about the huge blow that 9/11 was to the cause: "When that happened we were completely overshadowed. We took ourselves pretty seriously, but these guys were prepared to go a whole lot further than us." Is this really the scale you want to step on to? If brute force determines the winner, then in the end there is no winner at all.

The law and ... trespass

If you don't have permission to be on someone's property, for instance in a garden, a field or a factory, then you are trespassing. If you are adamant that you will not move – for example, if you have decided that you are going to plonk a protest camp there – the correct way for the owner to remove you is through the civil court system. Trespass is a civil wrong rather than a criminal offence, which means the police don't usually get involved.

In certain situations you have implied permission to be on land – for example, when a postman walks from a garden gate to a person's front door, he is not trespassing.

However, sometimes that permission may be withdrawn. Inside a coffee house, for example, you have implied permission to sit on the seating provided and drink your cappuccino – in the broadest possible sense, to use the premises as intended. If, however, you refused to leave when the staff wanted to close up, you would be trespassing – your permission to be there would have been withdrawn. Likewise, if you drop into your town hall on an open day you have implied permission to enter all of the rooms that have been prepared for visitors. However, if you scale the side of the hall and unfurl a banner from the roof, you have stepped outside the limits of that permission. Again, for both of these situations, if those in charge of the premises wanted to remove you, the correct method would be through the civil courts.

This is not how it always works in practice. In practice, if you stage a sit-down protest on someone else's property or stand on the roof chanting clever slogans, the person in charge of the property is likely to call the police. The police may use creative methods to try to get rid of you – for example, they may claim that you have caused or are causing criminal damage, and arrest you in order to remove you, or negotiate with you that they will not arrest you if you call it a day.

There are two main criminal offences associated with trespass of which protestors should be aware. The Criminal Justice and Public Order Act 1994 made it an offence (known as aggravated trespass) to trespass on land with the intention of intimidating, obstructing or disrupting any lawful activities there. This was principally intended to be used against hunt saboteurs but can be applied to a wide range of protest activities. The basis of the offence – that the defendant's activity should merely be "intended to" have a disruptive or intimidatory effect – gives wide scope to the police to intervene. They have powers under the same act to direct you to leave, and ignoring their orders is a criminal offence. These offences would be tried in a magistrates court, and if found guilty you could face three months in prison, a fine of £2,500, or both.

Interestingly, however, lawyers have recently decided that aggravated trespass only applies outdoors. The original law was framed to deal with hunt sabs and ravers, and only applied if the offenders were trespassing on land "in the open air". But in 2003 a clause was added to the Anti Social Behaviour Act which removed these words from the original legislation. And later – because, for complicated reasons, the removal of those words still did not make the situation entirely clear - an "explanatory note" was added stating that aggravated trespass now applied within office buildings. But the House of Lords recently decided that "explanatory notes" are not legislation because they come from the government, rather than from Parliament: Where possible you should always refer to the original legislation. All this emerged in a case of aggravated trespass in October 2009, where activists had got into a Kingsnorth building contractor's offices and superglued or D-locked themselves to the front door and to the stairs. After much to-ing and fro-ing, the judge agreed that the law was too ambiguous and dismissed the case.

The Public Order Act 1986, meanwhile, created offences related to "trespassory assemblies". If the local chief of police believes that someone intends to hold an assembly in a place where the public have limited or no right of access, he can apply to the local district council for an order prohibiting assemblies in that area for up to four days. Organising or taking part in such an assembly, if you know it has been banned, is an offence. You would again be tried in a magistrates court, and the penalties are the same as for aggravated trespass. Moreover, if you are on your way to such an assembly, a police officer can direct you not to proceed in that direction. The same penalties apply for failure to obey.

The last relevant bit of trespass law is concerned with the Serious Organised Crime and Police Act 2005, which has made a criminal offence of "trespassing on a designated site" and has a drastic effect on the legality of scaling buildings, unfurling banners or, say, throwing purple powder over the prime minister in the House of Commons. Sites may be "designated" by the government if they belonging to the crown or designation is in the interests of national security. Naturally, prime targets for protests, such as the Houses of Parliament and military bases, have been designated. Other sites designated more recently include most of the Royal properties, 10 Downing Street, the MoD main building, and a few other government buildings. The penalty for trespassing here is a fine of up to £5,000 and/or 51 weeks in prison. Your only defence is to prove that you did not know the site was designated.

... invasions and sit-ins

Right, so you're going to get in there and make your point, and then get straight out again. Or stay. You can't make your mind up. While you're thinking about that, here are the legal issues. Location is very important: if you are on public land, then as long as you are not obstructing the public highway, or causing damage, or harassing anyone, or on one of the designated sites (see above) you are within your rights. If you are planning to enter a building, the situation changes somewhat. If you need to use force in any way, you may be guilty of aggravated trespass or criminal damage. If, however, you enter in a peaceful way, do not harass anyone and remain polite throughout, then you are only committing a civil offence, so the police, strictly speaking, should not get involved. Although they may still be called in and may still carry you out of there, they are very unlikely to charge you: it would be up to the owners of the buildings to pursue you in the civil courts. And that happens very, very rarely.

There are a couple of exceptions to this; under the Criminal Justice and Immigration Act 2008 it's a criminal offence to cause a nuisance to an NHS member of staff. And under the Criminal Law Act 1977 it's a criminal offence to trespass in embassies and consular premises, or the private residences of diplomatic staff. (Also see "designated sites" above.)

It's also worth noting that under the Public Meeting Act 1908 it's unlawful to act in a "disorderly manner" in order to disrupt a lawful public meeting. Moreover, if you do this and then refuse to give your name and address when police ask, they can arrest you.

... and blockades

Blockading – trying to physically stop anything getting in or out of a site – is straightforwardly illegal. Obstructing the highway in any way is a crime under the Highways Act 1980. If the road is private, that will not apply, but chaining yourself across it could be considered to be disrupting business – and hence aggravated trespass. Breach of the peace is also a charge that is popular with police, and was used frequently during the year-long blockade of Faslane, the Scottish Trident base. You could also potentially be prosecuted under the Harassment Act 1997 – brought in as a measure against stalkers this Act is increasingly being used against protestors in many circumstances beyond blockades. A private individual or company needs to apply for an injunction to prevent the protestor, say, entering a specific area around their property on the grounds that you may cause distress or physical damage: if you break the injunction you will be committing a criminal offence. It has been used against animal rights protestors, and the British Airports Authorities tried to use it to stop protestors approaching Heathrow during the 2007 Climate Camp.

... lock-ons

When it comes to lock-ons, you're mostly likely to get arrested for criminal damage (criminal damage for say, the smallest of small scratches caused by whatever you're using to lock on) and taken away to interrupt the protest, but it is unlikely that you will be charged once at the police station. You may also get arrested for aggravated trespass, although – as we saw in the section about aggravated trespass – you may not get convicted if you are indoors.

... asbos

if you make yourself a big enough nuisance, your targets may ask the courts to grant an anti-social behaviour order against you. This would lay down terms for your behaviour; if you breached these, you could be prosecuted. Several animal rights activists have had asbos imposed on them, preventing them from going near the Huntingdon Life Sciences laboratory or from contacting the company's owners, shareholders or employees.

But don't despair: judges do throw out applications. In 2005 Lindis Percy, an anti-war campaigner who has been arrested over 150 times for peaceful protests inside or outside US air bases, was convicted of five offences of obstructing traffic outside the US National Security Agency's electronic eavesdropping base at Menwith Hill in Yorkshire. But the judge refused to grant an asbo, on the grounds that Percy's behaviour had not been threatening or insulting. The courts, he said, "ought not to allow anti-social behaviour orders to be used as a club to beat down the expression of legitimate comment".

... terrorism

What is a terrorist? This is one of the trickiest, most thorny of legal issues, with no answer likely any time soon. As a Liberty response to a government review of the legal definition of terrorism points out: "The United Nations member states have failed to agree on a single definition, which is perhaps unsurprising as one publication on the subject identified 109 different definitions of terrorism at the time it was written".

The famous aphorism "one man's terrorist is another man's freedom fighter" hints at the root of the problem: a definition of a terrorist is effectively a political definition. And in recent years in the UK that has come to seem truer than is entirely comfortable.

The old UK definition of terrorism used to be "acts of persons acting on behalf of, or in connection with, any organisation which carries out activities directed towards the overthrowing or influencing, by force or violence, of her majesty's government in the UK or any other government de jure or de facto". But in the late 90s Blair's New Labour decided that this was no longer enough. In 1998 the Home Office published a consultation paper setting out its proposals for new terrorism legislation. "The current definition of terrorism is too restrictive," it said and went on to list groups it wished to include in a broader definition, such as animal rights groups and environmental rights activists. "Last year, for example, more than 800 incidents were recorded by the Animal Rights National Index (ARNI). These included attacks on abattoirs, laboratories, breeders, hunts, butchers, chemists, doctors, vets, furriers, restaurants, supermarkets and other shops. Some of the attacks were minor but others were not. Thankfully no one was killed but people were injured and the total damage done in 1997 has been estimated at more than £1.8m ... Acts of serious violence against people and property have undoubtedly been committed in the UK by these domestic groups ... There is also the possibility that new groups espousing different causes will be set up and adopt violent methods to impose their will on the rest of society. In the United States, for example, there is an increasing tendency by individuals and groups to resort to terrorist methods. Some of those opposed to the USA's laws on abortion have bombed clinics and attacked, and, in a number of cases, killed doctors and nursing staff employed by them. Although there have been no comparable attacks in the United Kingdom, the possibility remains that some new group or individual could operate in this way in the future, threatening serious violence to people and property here."

And two years later the Terrorist Act 2000 re-defined terrorism. In UK law terrorism now means that "1. The action involves serious violence against a person, OR serious damage to property, OR endangers a person's life, other than that of the person committing the action, OR creates a serious risk to the health and safety of the public or a section of the public, OR is designed seriously to interfere with or seriously disrupt an electronic system AND 2. The use or threat is designed to influence the government or an international governmental organisation or to intimidate the public or section of the public OR involves the use of firearms or explosives AND 3. The use or threat is made for the purpose of advancing a political, religious, racial or ideological cause".

It is a broad-shaded definition into which, as many have pointed out, countless activities could be crammed. What, for example, is "serious damage to property"? Would a passionate opposition to genetically modified crops count as an ideological cause? Could the anti-GM campaigners who systematically ripped out crops have found themselves up on charges of terrorism? What does "a serious risk to the health or safety of the public" mean? Could shutting down a power station fit that definition?

And with this new broader definition has come corresponding new powers for the police, which they have used freely. Under section 44 of the Terrorism Act 2000 police were given new powers to stop and search "a person whom he reasonably suspects to be a terrorist to discover whether he has in his possession anything which may constitute evidence that he is a terrorist". And under sections 40-43 constables can arrest without warrant anyone they reasonably suspect of being a terrorist.

Further legislation followed; the Terrorism Act 2006, the Immigration, Asylum and Nationality Act 2006 which, according to Liberty, once again "created inappropriately broad offences and powers which were parasitic on the broad definition of terrorism contained in section 1 of TA2000". These include the offence of "encouraging terrorism", which could, it has been pointed out, include supporting resistance to oppressive governments overseas. Other offences created under the Terrorism legislation include belonging to a proscribed organization, fundraising for the purposes of terrorism, and failure to disclose any information relevant to an act of terrorism to the proper authorities.

The acts have since been used in various ways to inhibit protest. Police use section 44 freely during political conferences for example, most famously detaining the then 82-year-old Walter Wolfgang after he shouted "Nonsense" at Jack Straw during a 2005 speech about Iraq. According to Chris Atkins, director of the film Taking Liberties, police used this power 600 times during that particular conference, and to stop and search more than 35,000 individuals that year throughout the UK.

More recently, in 2009, Chris Kitchen was one of four activists stopped and searched by customs officials under schedule 7 of the Terrorist Act 2000, which allows border officials to stop, search and detain anyone they suspect to be in any way connected with terrorist activities. There is no requirement for "reasonable suspicion"; officials are free to use the powers exactly as they please. Kitchen was allowed to travel the following day, but environmental activists who were preparing to travel to Copenhagen in December 2009 made contingency plans in case they too were held up under this legislation.

Chapter Sixteen
Moving in

By now we know the routine. The success of any tactic depends on what you are trying to do with it, and squatting or occupation is no different. The twist with squatting, however, is the close, even symbiotic relationship that people all over the world have with their property. Those who believe that property is theft are a tiny minority: for most of us a happy family, a nice house and a bit of garden are the zenith of our dreams, and if as activists you fail to understand this and respect it, it may lead to the failure of your campaign. The public's sympathy and support will be important in determining how the local authority or government responds.

There are four main reasons that people move on to a bit of land or into an empty property: they have nowhere to live; they are protesting about the shortage of housing; they are protesting about some other issue, such as war or road-building or quarrying; or they want to set up their own space in which they can live the way they please. For the first reason, history has shown, squatting is of limited long-term usefulness. A handful of cases may be successful – in 1945 a wave of squatters took over empty army camps and were allowed to stay, and here and there in the years since an unusual local authority has handed over properties to long-term squatters – but the majority will sooner or later be evicted and back to square one.

In the short term squatting can be, of course, very useful although as a protest against a shortage of housing, it is effective only as long as the squatters retain the sympathy of the public. In both the 40s and the 70s the squatting movements had that to begin with, and then forfeited it – in the 70s, for example, as some of the squatters became more militant and the press decided that instead of heroically reoccupying empty houses, they were now blocking people on council waiting lists from getting homes. After that it all got a bit more adversarial, and far less effective as a protest tactic.

What about protest camps – squatting along the route of a planned road, for example? It's quite risky because, again, can you retain the sympathy of the local people? Camp Bling is a camp in Essex that has been erected in protest against the widening of Priory Crescent, one of the main roads into Southend-on-Sea. The camp is in a wee hiccup of land hooped by the road, which is full of slow-moving cars; the constant congestion is, of course, the reason Southend council wants to widen it. It's a noisy spot, and Shaun Quereshi, who was one of the group that set up the camp, says that the sound of the traffic drives some people mad, but he's kind of used to it now. Camp Bling has already won a big concession from the council, which has suggested leaving this particular bit of road and doing the widening a bit further up, though actually that just emphasises the daftness of the whole project: any road that is two lanes at one point and then one a bit further down is going to continue to suffer from congestion. Bling's inhabitants have said no: they're going to hold out for the project to be cancelled altogether.

They're a level-headed lot, and the camp has been set up thoughtfully with a big sign over the gate saying "Welcome", and a visitor's centre for passersby. Compared with some protest camps, which become very inward-looking and cliquey, this is a huge improvement. There is a clear set of rules, a strict no-drugs policy, and every weekend the activists have a stall in the town centre to make sure they stay in touch with what local people are thinking. As a result, although of course they get some hassle (one of their treehouses has been burned down), the council can't attack them for being nuisances and, according to Katherine Legge, one of the reporters on the Southend Echo, "because they put in a lot of work in the early days to ingratiate themselves with local people, they've had a lot of local support. People take stuff down to them, and families will go down there at the weekends with their kids to see if anything's going on." She points out, moreover, that it's beginning to look as if the road project is more or less permanently on hold.

Protest camps can work, in other words, if they're focused on a fairly soft target, and carefully handled. Then it becomes both expensive and embarrassing for the local authorities to remove them. "We worry about being a single-issue camp," says Quereshi, "but I think if we started jumping up and down shouting about climate change that would just put people off, and we need to keep them onside."

Why I fight

Jill Raymond
Veteran of the Greenham and Aldermaston peace camps

I was there at the beginning of Greenham, and me and a friend went up, right at the end, to help tow the last caravan away. When I think about Greenham and when I think about the camp that we have now at Aldermaston, the thing that comes to mind is community, being with people who feel the same way as you.

We went to Greenham because we just felt angry that the Americans were bringing nuclear weapons over here. It was a mixed camp to start with, but we got tired of dealing with drunk men from peace convoys looking for a fight with the police. A lot of us were lesbians and according to the soft end of the feminist movement at the time it was all right to be lesbian as long as you didn't talk about it. But at Greenham we had a society where we could just be out and that was fine. Men were welcome during daylight hours but not at night.

We did feel vulnerable sometimes. We used to get squaddies out of uniform coming to beat us up, and vigilantes from the local towns, or prowlers around the shit pits in the woods, so you always wanted someone to come with you. And it could be absolutely freezing – you would wake up with your boots frozen on.

After the Greenham camp had been dismantled, several of us carried on coming to Aldermaston, which is about 12 miles away. There's a camp once a month. It's very different from Greenham, though: we're all over 50 and we worry a lot about how to get younger women involved. At Greenham we used to get runaways from all sorts of domestic problems and we could help them out with the camp dole, but you wouldn't be able to sign on and give a peace camp as your address nowadays.

I travel a lot now, but whenever I get back this is the place I come to touch base. It's a cultural thing for me. I feel at home sitting by the fence, cooking in the open, in an illegal encampment. It's exhausting, this endless campaign, but you have to stand up and be counted.

But my goodness, you need a lot of commitment to do this. The Bling bunch are the most respectable protest campers you can imagine – they almost all have full-time jobs, and some have flats in the area but have chosen to live here instead until the battle is won – and that is how they've done so well. Tougher targets – such as military bases – are a different proposition altogether. There is nothing like the number of protest camps now that we saw in the 90s: it may sound romantic, but doing without hot water and electricity and living in tents or benders palls quickly for most.

What about the fourth reason to squat – to take over territory in order to set up a space for your own way of life? In some ways this is the most significant of all of them, and in recent years this kind of squatting has seen a global renaissance. The ideas of land reform and property redistribution have obviously been at the heart of most radical schools of political thought, but now, after the dumbstruck silence caused by the collapse of communism, they are shyly resurfacing. And this brings us full circle back to the English civil war and the Diggers. Gerard Winstanley, the Diggers' theorist, was one of the great visionaries in political history: he has been called the father of communism, but also the father of anarchism. The historian Christopher Hill records the time when, told that his beliefs "will destroy all government and all our ministry and religion", Winstanley replied coolly: "It is very true," His tactic was extremely simple: while turbulence rocked the country during the second eruption of war, on April 1 1649 Winstanley and his comrades began to dig up waste land in St George's Hill in the parish of Walton-on-Thames.

Squatting had been practised for centuries, but not as part of a unified political theory. Winstanley saw that one third of the country's land was barren waste, which the landowners would not permit the poor to cultivate, and he declared: "If the waste land of England were manured by her children, it would become in a few ideas the richest, the strongest and [most] flourishing land in the world." The Diggers attempted, for a brief time, to turn common land into homes and vegetable plots, but their tiny movement was harassed and evicted by landowners and courts, they were moved from on towns and, by one report, forced to hand their children over to the parish. By 1651 they had given up. Winstanley became a Quaker.

Nearly 350 years later, the Zapatistas took a leaf out of Winstanley's book and occupied (by force at first, although they soon laid down their arms) territories in Chiapas, the southernmost state of Mexico. To recap a story that you will probably have heard, on January 1 1994, as Mexico celebrated the new year, the guerillas finally came out of the jungle after a decade of training. A friend of mine was in San Cristobal de las Casas (one of the villages they invaded) that night; he vividly remembers stepping outside the bar to clear his head from the New Year's celebrations, and seeing this silent line of balaclavaed figures, rifles slung over their backs, passing across the head of the road on their way to the town hall. While the officials tried to understand what was going on, the peasant forces took control of four towns.

I spent seven months in Chiapas in 1997; it is the most fascinating, beautiful, aggravating place you can imagine. As a westerner the slow pace of life initially drove me mad, but then it became more normal; harder to adjust to was the reluctance of the villagers in Zapatista territory to ever directly answer a question about politics or fighting or the future or anything much at all. (The Zapatistas' main spokesman at that time was Subcomandante Marcos, a wonderful writer but in love with rhetorical flourishes. Sometimes you wish he'd just spit it out.) But the timing of their uprising revealed their target: they came out of the jungle just as Mexico implemented the North American Free Trade Agreement with America and Canada. What the Zapatistas were after was an autonomous space, a place where they could hang on to the smallholdings that would be unviable in this new free trade world. A place where they could live the way they wanted to.

And this idea, of a space in which you can live as you like, rather than as the global markets dictate, has been a beacon for activists all over the world. Throughout Europe and the US there had already been radical social movements – the 60s, 70s and 80s had seen a variety of experiments with communal living, some successful, some just hilarious or awful, and at the same time environmental direct action was exploding – but the Zapatistas immediately became a focal point of this energy. The socialists, running out of ideas, hoped that this could be a new possibility. More importantly, the Zapatista anxiety about globalisation became the centre of the anti-capitalist movement. The Chiapaneca Indians, after all, had been living under imperialist rule since the Spaniards arrived. Their state, with its fantastic mineral resources, had been exploited for decades and remained the poorest in Mexico, with fewer teachers and nurses than any other. The Indians, in their own country, were marginalised by a rich elite, and they were well aware that the free trade agreement would just make everything worse.

By 1997, when I was there, the Zapatistas were negotiating with the Mexican government. They were occupying several tracts of land, which were basically under their control: that meant no drinking, for starters. Village decisions, taken in the consulta, had to be unanimous.

Land was redistributed, and though the communities were still poor, they regarded themselves as autonomous. The village where I stayed – La Realidad, deep in the heart of the Lacandon jungle – was a quiet, dreamy place, where few people knew their birthday or age. The Zapatista army was believed to be somewhere nearby and the young men who played football on the pitch every evening wore suspiciously sturdy boots. The Mexican army drove through every day, as if otherwise we would forget they were nearby. The food was basic – eggs, beans, tortillas, coffee and Coca-Cola – and the huts were earth-floored. We all slept in hammocks and washed in the river, and the sense that the Zapatista command was pulling the strings from within the jungle nearby was extremely unsettling. But at the same time there was a proper schoolhouse, with a motley library of books contributed by visitors over the years, and the children could all read and write. And the marches I attended with the villagers made it clear that this was not puppetry: it was a fierce, fearsome demand directly from the Indians for respect and independence.

A year earlier the Zapatistas had held the first encuentro: thousands of people from all over the world travelled into the jungle and talked about ideas for the future, and then met again in Spain the following year. These meetings were the seedbed for the World Social Forum and the European Social Forum: they put thousands of activists from around the world in contact with each other, and have led to events such as the global street party on June 18 1999. Is there a global social movement as a result? It's way too diverse to be called one movement, but undeniably there are connections between lots of small movements, and one of the demands that is ringing out loudest is for some kind of space that is safe from the global market, from the inflexible rule of the free market. The Via Campesina international peasant alliance's food sovereignty movement, which demands the right to control one's own food supply, to decide how and where food is produced and sold, is pretty much the modern-day equivalent of Winstanley's arguments.

There is a small British codicil to this story. I have not talked much about anarchists in this book, but in the early 21st century it's interesting to reflect that one of the only radical political theories that continues to have some vitality (poor old communism, still struggling to get back off the ropes after Stalin) is anarchy. In the years during and since the Zapatista uprising, the anarchist movement has apparently given up on bringing down the state, and focused more on building its own societies. The consensus system, on which the Zapatistas operate, has also been perfected by anarchist activists: energy has been centred on working out how best to live cooperatively, and it has been accepted that a small community needs to agree a set of basic rules, needs to make compromises among its members, in order to survive.

The anarchist Matthew Herbert says: "We needed a break, basically. We wanted somewhere we could just relax, instead of being evicted all the time and moved on. So we took a few years out to build the social centres." It's not clear, of the 30 or so centres that the anarchists now run in the UK, how many are squatted; a good percentage, however, are collectively owned. After a whole wave of political bookshops closed down, centres such as the Cowley Club in Brighton are starting their own bookshops. They also provide useful space for meetings, there's usually some sort of event on the board, and some offer legal advice or even emotional support. As one activist explained to me: "In the 90s we were great at developing all the hard skills – bolting ourselves to diggers, that sort of thing. But this decade we've focused on some of the soft stuff too – the social centres, or dealing with activist burnout."

Community, local control, collective decision-making: these ideas have rich possibilities for the future, in a world that will no doubt change radically over the next century. Funnily enough, Pierre-Joseph Proudhon, author of the famous anarchist maxim "property is theft", also stated that "property is freedom". No reason not to think that both are true, really.

The law and ... squatting

There are two provisions of law that make squatting possible. Section six of the Criminal Law Act 1977 is all about "offences relating to entering and remaining on property" and makes it a criminal offence for a landlord – or other person entitled to live in the property, such as a tenant – to use violence for the purposes of gaining entry when he knows that there are people present. In Northern Ireland section 6 doesn't apply so this would not be particularly useful. Violence in the section is defined as being against people or property – so breaking the locks or breaking the door down is included, as is dragging squatters out forcibly. For this reason, squatters who know their stuff will always make sure that there is at least one person present in the property and often place a "legal warning" on the front door stating that it is occupied at all times. Section six was diluted a bit by an amendment in the Criminal Justice and Public Order Act 1994, which added provisions about "protected intending occupiers" and "displaced residential occupiers". Basically, if squatters are told that the building is required for residential occupation by its rightful inhabitants, they have to get out or risk being arrested. Bang. But this only applies to premises that genuinely are used for residential purposes. A building marked for development by a property company could therefore be squatted without this provision coming into play.

The other provision of law that relates to squatters is section one of the Protection From Eviction Act 1977, titled "unlawful eviction and harassment of occupier". Essentially, it builds upon the provisions of the Criminal Law Act 1977 listed above – it makes it an offence for a landlord (or anybody else) to unlawfully deprive a squatter (or anyone on the premises) of his home, or to do acts likely "to interfere with the peace or comfort" of the squatter. This section was not aimed at squatters! It was introduced to protect tenants from unfair landlords; however, the definition of "residential occupier" in the section is broad enough to include squatters. The law in Northern Ireland is more narrowly drawn and squatters are not covered.

There is one further thing that squatters should be aware of: using services such as water, electricity and gas without paying could lead to a prosecution for theft. Squatters should inform utilities that they are the new residents and set up a new account, bearing in mind that it is probably wise to do so without mentioning that they are squatting.

... protest camps

If you're setting up a protest camp, you need to know whether you're on public or private land, as different laws will apply to you. If you're camping on private land, then the owner can ask the local authority to direct you to leave – but this only applies, under sections 77–80 of the Criminal Justice and Public Order Act 1994, if you're in wheeled vehicles. Otherwise he may turn to another section of the act: number 61 states that if any of the campers "has caused damage to the land or to property on the land or used threatening, abusive or insulting words or behaviour towards the occupier, a member of his family or an employee or agent of his", they can be all be told to leave. And failure to obey the direction is a criminal offence.

If you're on public land, the wheeled vehicle thing applies again. But you're more likely to be caught out by "bylaws" – rules that apply to a specific area. They are generally made by the local authority, but can be also made by the secretary of state and apply to areas such as military bases, so campers should find out from the relevant local authority what bylaws affect the land they have their sights on. Subtly, obviously. A whole new set of bylaws was brought in recently in Aldermaston, where a women's peace camp has been running once a month since the 80s. These new bylaws create a long list of prohibited activities, prescribing, among other things, that no person shall: enter or leave the protected areas except by way of an official entrance or exit; remain in the protected areas after having been directed to leave; obstruct a lawful user acting in the proper exercise of his duty within the protected areas; take any photographs of any person or thing within the protected areas; make any false statement, either orally or in writing, or employ any other form of misrepresentation in order to obtain entry to any part of the protected areas; attach any thing to, or place any thing over any wall, fence, structure or other surface surrounding or within the protected areas; or deface any sign, wall, fence, structure or other surface within the protected areas. They're pretty typical of the bylaws made for military bases around the UK, which are used to try and remove protestors from land. The campers fight back in the courts, lodging counter-claims against eviction and hoping that landowners will not kick them out until the case and any appeals have been decided, for fear of having the evictions declared unlawful.

Chapter Seventeen
The argument against campaigning – and why you should ignore it

So what is the point of all this? The earth won't permit us to keep on handing out rights and privileges left, right and centre to people who forget they have them. Mankind shows no sign of getting nicer, even after millennia of effort, there's still plenty of torturing and war-mongering and murdering going on, and moreover the planet is dropping to pieces around us. Really, why not face the fact that you just can't win?

All right, let's take the moment when your campaign has succeeded. The local council has refused the supermarket planning application, or the corporation has promised to look into more environmentally friendly ways of generating electricity, or the government has agreed to draft a bill making it illegal to eat fish on Wednesdays. You're going on holiday tomorrow, you never want to see a D-lock again, and if anyone asks you to sign a petition you'll laugh in their face.

Drink the champagne quickly, because if history teaches us anything, it is that these results don't stick. The supermarket announces that it will appeal, the corporation produces a meaning-less report and does absolutely nothing, the government's bill is watered down into uselessness. The guys with the money and power, it seems, will always win in the end. If you were a defeatist, you might conclude that this campaigning business is a mug's game.

Let's glance at a few moments in the history of one particular cause, child labour in factories, to see how this works. From the 1750s onwards factories were springing up all over Britain. Mill owners had already realised that children were particularly useful because of their small fingers, and because they could be paid less, and so they were herded in through the factory gates in their thousands and forced to work shifts of 10, 12, 15 hours. The historian and campaigner EP Thompson tells the story of a boy found standing asleep with his arms full of wool and beaten awake by the factory overseer: he worked 17 hours that day, was carried home by his father, and died in the night. It was a brutal, horrific time in our history: no wonder the Fabians formed on the promise that they would face civil war rather than another century of suffering such as that of the industrial revolution. For the whole of the 19th century an array of campaigners fought desperately to get children out of the factories, despite slanders and attacks from the mill-owners, and the threat that they would undermine the basis of British industry, through a succession of compromised or watered-down Factory Acts. In 1842 it was made illegal for children under 13 to work more than six-and-a-half hours. In 1874 the minimum working age was raised to nine.

As time went by, however, other countries industrialised and shoved their children through the factory doors. And now? Has child labour been stamped out? No: you could say that rich countries with strict laws and the will to enforce them have simply exported the misery to new manufacturing centres, such as Bangladesh, Uzbekistan and China. An undercover investigation for Channel 4 in 2006, for example, revealed that in Bangladesh children as young as 12 were employed by the garment industry, making clothes for well-known western retailers. Most campaigners, at some point as they watch a report like this, find themselves wondering whether there is really any point carrying on.

But the thing is that most campaigners do what they do not because they think that by next week they'll have achieved a perfect world, but because if hope is lined up against greed, they'd rather be on this side of the line. They believe that the world will not be made perfect, but may at least be made a little better. Doggedness: after passion, this is the single most necessary quality for any campaigner.

As the anti-sweatshop campaigner Martin Hearson says, "If we weren't here, who knows what the world would be like?"

As for passion ... Here in the west in the 21st century it has finally become clear that as humans we do not have natural rights, that there is no built-in moral code or natural virtuousness upon which we can draw, as Rousseau believed in his early years. And for many people there is no god or king who can dictate these things, there is no master race (not down my way anyway) or life after death. In fact, in the ongoing argument in the west about the origins of morality, the "Why?" of humanity, the sociobiologists such as Richard Dawkins, who argue that our lives are about nothing more than the survival and preservation of genes, seem to be taking the lead. Their vision of a world where everyone scrabbles to get what is theirs has become so firmly entrenched as a rationale for rampant capitalism, for the free market and all the exploitation it entails, that it seems harder and harder to suggest an alternative vision.

Obviously protest and campaigning have their roles to play in this particular world view. If someone else is going to get the right to – say – receive a huge pension, we need to make sure we don't miss out. It's pretty obvious from what we've already seen that the rights for which we campaign are often for our own benefit: they make our situation better, although perhaps at the expense of a king or a dictator or two. After all, society is basically a game of tug-of-war around a huge circular tablecloth, and some of the teams are huge and brawny, and others are small but determined, and everyone is just pulling as hard as they can to get the tablecloth to come over a little way in their direction. And "our" side is absolutely essential. If there were no pulling from this side, the strong guys opposite would just roll the tablecloth up and do it all their way. It's all about self-interest, protecting your own little patch.

And cooperation, it turns out, is all part of the survival strategy too: in fact, according to a computer game that scientists have been playing for about 30 years now, it's the best strategy of all. The game is based on the "prisoner's dilemma", a classic riddle that explores the choice between cooperation and competition. Two criminals have been put into separate cells and the police are pressuring them for confessions. There is very little evidence against them, so if both prisoners keep quiet they will each get off with a year in jail. If one of them informs on the other, he will go free and the other will get 10 years. But if they both snitch, they will each get three years. Suppose you find yourself in this situation; can you trust your accomplice to keep his promise not to betray you? What should you do?

In the 70s, a political scientist called Robert Axelrod set up a computer world that would play infinite games of prisoner's dilemma, and asked other scientists to submit strategies. The winner was a very simple routine (only five lines long) called Tit for Tat, which began by keeping silent, then did whatever the other player had done on the previous encounter. So if both prisoners did the honourable thing and held their tongues – in other words cooperated – they would settle into a happy and mutually beneficial relationship. If the other grassed, then Tit for Tat would grass too, and continue to do so until the other reformed, at which point it would return to benevolent behaviour. Tit for Tat vanquished all comers. Cooperating, onc can conclude, is the way forward. Looking after each other, watching out for the weaker members of society, is not just a sucker's reflex – it's a winning strategy in our society.

Is that all? Well, the evolutionary psychologists might add in a search for higher social status (which gets you more and better food and sex, basically). They might suggest that in protesting against the uneven distribution of wealth in this society we are expressing our ancient disapproval of hoarding, a taboo in many hunter-gatherer societies such as the Inuits. They would suggest that in trying to prevent an airport being built in our back garden, we're displaying the same territoriality as any animal.

But there is one form of human behaviour that does seem to floor them time and again, and it gives me hope that there is, perhaps, a bit more to all this than a robotic struggle to get what's ours. Matt Ridley, who specialises in writing about sociobiology when he's not resigning as non-executive chairman of Northern Rock, comes up against this problem in his book The Origins of Virtue, where he attempts in one rushed passage to explain the problem of altruism, of "acts of genuine goodness", such as flying to Rwanda to bathe sick orphans in a refugee camp. How to account for a woman who commits these acts even though they are not "selfish or rational"? Ridley can suggest only that "she is prey to sentiments that are designed for another purpose: to elicit trust by demonstrating a capacity for altruism." Robert Wright, whose book The Moral Animal you might imagine would deal with this problem, cannot cope at all with the issue of morality in a post-Darwinian world, and decides that "this is a deep and murky question that (readers may be relieved to hear) will not be rigorously addressed in this book." And Richard Dawkins himself, the head cheerleader for the sociobiologists, has come to believe, in contemplating genuinely selfless, apparently un-Darwinian friends of his, that "super-niceness" as he calls it, is "a misfiring, even a perversion of the Darwinian take on niceness … From a rational-choice point of view, or from a Darwinian point of view, human super-niceness is just plain dumb." He is aware, some-where in the depths of his mind, that this is the sort of statement that makes people look at him pityingly and want to pat him on the head and ask about his childhood, so he adds: "Well, if that's a perversion, it's the kind of perversion we need to encourage and spread."

But from my non-scientific point of view, these seem extremely inadequate explanations for the fact of altruism, for the love that humans clearly feel for each other, for the things we are prepared to do for each other. It's an odd blindness about humanity that the sociobiologists seem to share. Have they never been tempted to chain themselves up with four other people in a giant pair of Y-fronts made out of D-locks and blockade an army base with a huge sign saying War Is Pants? Have they never stood in a huge crowd of trade union-ists singing along at the top of their voices to Billy Bragg's Waiting for the Great Leap Forwards? Have they never dressed up as a rainforest and spent a day lying on the pavement outside their local McDonald's? If I had to hazard a guess, I would say ... no.

In 1975 Omar Cabezas, a young Sandinista activist in Nicaragua, went into the mountains to become a guerrilla. His account of the training is tragic and hilarious – having expected to become part of a huge secret army, instead he arrives at a camp where there are just a handful of men. He and eight comrades endure rain, sleeping in hammocks, being rubbed raw by their rifles, being eaten alive by mosquitoes "to be like Che, to be like Che". That is the refrain that runs through his head every day, during fights and exhaustion and near-mutiny. The Sandinista guerrillas are trying to form Che's New Man – "an open, unegotistical man, no longer petty, a tender man who sacrifices himself for others, a man who gives everything for others, who suffers when others suffer and who also laughs when others laugh". Is it really possible that this idealism, this desire to serve other human beings, is nothing more than "misfiring"?

Anyone who has ever been to a political meeting will know that status-seeking is rampant in grassroots politics, that campaigners can grind a meeting into the ground with a four-hour discussion about clause 10 of the statutes, that everyone wants to do something different and that half of them will promise to do something and then forget or not bother. If you want to back up a belief that human beings are selfish and only out for themselves, and that this is the natural order of things, I've been at meetings that are like cartoons of this kind of behaviour. But ...

But, we've also seen the man standing in front of a line of tanks in Tiananmen Square. We've watched the monks walking through the streets of Burma with their peaceful message of defiance for the military junta. We've marched to stop our governments prosecuting an illegal war against Iraq – to stop innocent people whom we had never met being killed. How does any of this benefit us socially? What if in reality humans are more than just a bundle of selfish instincts left over from the savannah? What if, out of that bundle of nerves and genes an ability to be occasionally truly altruistic has arisen? What if this is what Jesus Christ, that original promoter of extreme altruism, was on about all along? Aneurin Bevan said that "the capacity for emotional concern for human life is the most significant quality of a civilised human being". At its best, protesting – like the Scottish factory workers who strike in solidarity with Chilean prisoners, or the anti-war protestors who gather in their millions to plead with the government, or the eco-loonies living in elaborate spiders' webs in the treetops – is an act of creativity, an act of solidarity, an act of love, a gift that is given freely. For me, protest is right up there with a kiss and a poem as part of the hope for humanity.

Protest phone book

Animal rights

Animal Aid
The Old Chapel
Bradford Street
Tonbridge
Kent TN9 1AW
www.animalaid.org.uk
01732 364 546

British Union of Anti-Vivisectionists
16a Crane Grove
London N7 8NN
www.buav.org
020 7700 4888

Compassion in World Farming
River Court
Mill Lane
Godalming
Surrey GU7 1EZ
www.ciwf.org.uk
01483 521 950

Peta
PO Box 36678
London SE1 1YE
www.peta.org.uk
020 7357 9229

Viva!
8 York Court
Wilder Street
Bristol BS2 8QH
www.viva.org.uk
0117 944 1000

Boycotts, ethical shopping and solidarity

Baby Milk Action
34 Trumpington Street
Cambridge CB2 1QY
www.babymilkaction.org
01223 464420

Boycott Israeli Goods
www.bigcampaign.org
0207 700 6192

Burma Campaign UK
28 Charles Square
London N1 6HT
www.burmacampaign.org.uk
020 7324 4710

**Campaign for the
Accountability of American
Bases**
59 Swarcliffe Road
Harrogate HG1 4QZ
www.caab.org.uk
01423 884076/07949 897 904

**Colombia Solidarity
Campaign**
PO Box 8446
London N17 6NZ
www.colombiasolidarity.org.uk

Corporate Watch
c/o Freedom Press
Angel Alley
84b Whitechapel High Street
London E1 7QX
www.corporatewatch.org
020 7426 0005

Cuba Solidarity
c/o UNITE Woodberry
218 Green Lanes
London N4 2HB
www.cuba-solidarity.org.uk
020 8800 0155

Ecolabelling
http://ecolabelling.org
01604 682 6673

Ethical Consumer
Unit 21
41 Old Birley Street
Manchester M15 5RF
www.ethicalconsumer.org
0161 226 2929

Free Tibet Campaign
28 Charles Square
London N1 6HT
www.freetibet.org
020 7324 4605

The Haiti Support Group
www.haitisupport.gn.apc.org

Iraq Solidarity Campaign
www.iraqsolidaritycampaign.blog
spot.com

**The Kurdish Human Rights
Project**
11 Guilford Street
London WC1N 1DH
www.khrp.org
020 7405 3835

London Citizens
112 Cavell Street
London E1 2JA
www.londoncitizens.org.uk
020 7043 9881

No Music Day
contact@nomusicday.com
www.nomusicday.com

**Palestine Solidarity
Campaign**
Box BM PSA
London WC1N 3XX
www.palestinecampaign.org
020 7700 6192

**Scottish Palestine Solidarity
Campaign**
c/o Peace & Justice Centre
Princes Street
Edinburgh EH2 4BJ
www.scottishpsc.org.uk
0131 620 0052

Western Sahara Campaign
www.wsahara.org.uk
01974 282575

Campaign help

**10 Downing Street
e-petitions**
http://petitions.pm.gov.uk

Directory for Social Change
24 Stephenson Way
London NW1 2DP
www.dsc.org.uk
020 7391 4800

Funderfinder
65 Raglan Road
Leeds LS2 9DZ
www.funderfinder.org.uk

**Fundraising Standards
Board**
1st Floor
89 Albert Embankment
London SE1 7TP
www.frsb.org.uk
0845 402 5442

Gambling Commission
Victoria Square House
Victoria Square
Birmingham B2 4BP
www.gamblingcommission.gov.uk
0121 230 6666

Gopetition
www.gopetition.com

Government Funding
www.governmentfunding.org.uk

Grants Online
PO Box 5965
20 Merryfield Close
Verwood BH31 9AB
www.grantsonline.org.uk
01202 813452

GuideStar UK
Queens House
55-56 Lincoln's Inn Fields
London WC2A 3LJ
http://guidestar.org.uk
020 7831 0660

Institute of Fundraising
Park Place
12 Lawn Lane
London SW8 1UD
www.institute-of-
fundraising.org.uk
020 7840 1000

**National Association of
Voluntary and Community
Action**
The Tower
2 Furnival Square
Sheffield S1 4QL
www.navca.org.uk
0114 278 6636

**National Council for
Voluntary Organisations**
Regent's Wharf
8 All Saints Street
London N1 9RL
www.ncvo-vol.org.uk
020 7713 6161/0800 2798 798

**National Social Marketing
Centre**
20 Grosvenor Gardens
London SW1W ODH
www.nsmcentre.org.uk
020 7799 1900

People and Planet
51 Union Street
Oxford OX4 1JP
www.peopleandplanet.org
01865 245678

Planning Aid
6th Floor Newater House
11 Newhall Street
Birmingham B3 3NY
www.planningaid.rtpi.org.uk
0121 214 2900

Seeds for Change
96 Church St
Lancaster LA1 1TD
www.seedsforchange.org.uk
0845 330 7583

Volunteering England
Regents Wharf
8 All Saints Street
London N1 9RL
www.volunteering.org.uk
0845 305 6979

Women's Institute
104 New Kings Road
London SW6 4LY
www.thewi.org.uk
020 7371 9300

Environment

Biodynamic Association (UK)
The Biodynamic Agricultural Association
(BDAA)
Painswick Inn Project
Gloucester Street
Stroud
Gloucestershire GL5 1QG
www.biodynamic.org.uk
01453 759 501

British Wind Energy Association
Greencoat House
Francis Street
London SW1P 1DH
www.bwea.com
020 7901 3000

Campaign Against Climate Change
Top Floor
5 Caledonion Road
London N1 9DX
www.campaigncc.org
020 7833 9311

Campaign for Better Transport
16 Waterside
44-48 Wharf Road
London N1 7UX
www.bettertransport.org.uk
020 7566 6480

Campaign for the Protection of Rural England
CPRE National Office
128 Southwark Street
London SE1 0SW
www.cpre.org.uk/home
020 7981 2800

Campaign for Real Events
www.c-realevents.demon.co.uk

Camp Bling
priory_parklife@yahoo.co.uk
www.savepriorypark.org

Camp for Climate Action
Cornerstone Resource Centre
16 Sholebroke Avenue
Leeds LS7 3HB
www.climatecamp.org.uk
07594 521 290

Carbon Reduction Action Groups
www.carbonrationing.org.uk

Centre for Alternative Technology
Machynlleth
Powys
Wales SY20 9AZ
www.cat.org.uk
01654 705950

Clean Air in London
(Under the auspices of The Knightsbridge Association)
6 Montpelier Street
London SW7 1EZ
www.cleanairinlondon.org
020 7823 9103

Countryside Alliance
The Old Town Hall
367 Kennington Road
London SE11 4PT
www.countryside-alliance.org
020 7840 9200

Earth First!
www.earthfirst.org.uk/actionreports

Environmental Investigation Agency
62/63 Upper Street
London N1 0NY
www.eia-international.org
020 7354 7960

Forestry Stewardship Council
www.fsc.org/en

Friends of the Earth
26-28 Underwood Street
London N1 7JQ
www.foe.co.uk
020 7490 1555

Friends of the Earth Scotland
Thorn House
5 Rose Street
Edinburgh EH2 2PR
www.foe-scotland.org.uk
0131 243 2700

Friends of the Earth Cymru
33 Castle Arcade Balcony
Cardiff CF10 1BY
www.foe.co.uk/cymru/
029 2022 9577

Greenpeace
Canonbury Villas
London N1 2PN
www.greenpeace.org.uk
020 7865 8100

Groundwork
Lockside
5 Scotland Street
Birmingham B1 2RR
www.groundwork.org.uk
0121 236 8565

HACAN ClearSkies
PO Box 339
Twickenham TW1 2XF
www.hacan.org.uk
020 8876 0455

Low Impact Living Initiative
Redfield Community
Winslow
Bucks MK18 3LZ
www.lowimpact.org
01296 714184

Marine Conservation Society
Unit 3, Wolf Business Park
Alton Road
Ross-on-Wye
Herefordshire HR9 5NB
www.mcsuk.org
01989 566017

Marine Stewardship Council
3rd floor, Mountbarrow House
6-20 Elizabeth Street
London SW1W 9RB
www.msc.org
0207 811 3300

Plane Stupid
www.planestupid.com
07595 506673

Reclaim the Streets
http://rts.gn.apc.org

Rising Tide
62 Fieldgate Street
London E1 1ES
www.risingtide.org.uk
07708 794 665

Sea Shepherd Conservation Society
Sea Shepherd UK
Argyle House
1 Dee Road
Richmond-Upon-Thames
Surrey TW9 2JN
www.seashepherd.org

Soil Association
South Plaza
Marlborough Street
Bristol BS1 3NX
www.soilassociation.org
0117 314 5000

Soil Association Scotland
18C Liberton Brae
Tower Mains
Edinburgh EH16 6AE
www.soilassociationscotland.org
0131 666 2474

Stop Climate Chaos
The Grayston Centre
28 Charles Square
London N1 6HT
www.stopclimatechaos.org
020 7324 4622

Stop Stansted Expansion
PO Box 311
Takeley
Bishop's Stortford
Herts CM22 6PY
www.stopstanstedexpansion.com
01279 870558

Surfers Against Sewage
Unit 2
Wheal Kitty Workshops
St Agnes
Cornwall TR5 0RD
www.sas.org.uk
01872 555950

Sustrans
National Cycle Network Centre
2 Cathedral Square
College Green
Bristol BS1 5DD
www.sustrans.org.uk
0117 926 8893

This Land Is Ours
Chapter 7
The Potato Store
Flax Drayton Farm
South Petherton TA13
www.tlio.org.uk
01460 249 204

Transition Towns Network
www.transitiontowns.org
Two Moors Campaign
PO Box 132
Tiverton EX16 0AP
www.twomoorscampaign.co.uk
01884 881278/559

Women's Environmental Network
PO Box 30626
London E1 1TZ
www.wen.org.uk
020 7481 9004

Food and health

The Food Commission
94 White Lion Street
London
N1 9PF
www.foodmagazine.org.uk
020 7837 2250

Hyperactive Children's Support Group
71 Whyke Lane
Chichester
West Sussex PO19 7PD
www.hacsg.org.uk
01243 539966

Lake District Farmers
Diamond Buildings
Pennington Lane
Lindal-in-Furness
Cumbria LA12 0LA
01229 588299

Organic Farmers & Growers
www.organicfarmers.org.uk

The Organic Food Federation
31 Turbine Way
EcoTech Business Park
Swaffham
PE37 7XD
www.orgfoodfed.com
01760 720444

Scottish Organic Producers Association
SFQC
Royal Highland Centre
10th Avenue
Ingliston, Edinburgh EH28 8NF
www.sopa.org.uk
0131 335 6606

Soil Association
South Plaza
Marlborough Street
Bristol BS1 3NX
www.soilassociation.org
0117 314 5000

Sustain
94 White Lion Street
London N1 9PF
www.sustainweb.org
020 7837 1228

The Vegan Society
Donald Watson House
21 Hylton Street
Hockley
Birmingham B18 6HJ
www.vegansociety.com
0121 523 1730

Workers Beer Company
347 Garratt Lane
Earlsfield
London SW18 4DX
www.workersbeer.co.uk

Genetic modification

Genetic Engineering Network

c/o Caerhys Farm
Berea
St David's
Pembrokeshire SA62 6DX
www.geneticsaction.org.uk
01348 831 244

GM-Free Scotland

35 Hamilton Drive
Glasgow G12 8DW
www.gmfreescotland.net
0141 339 6913

GMWatch

c/o 26 Pottergate,
Norwich NR2 1DX
www.gmwatch.org
01603 624021

Independent bookshops, publishers and media

Bookmarks
1 Bloomsbury Street
London WC1B 3QE
www.bookmarks.uk.com
020 7637 1848

Freedom Press
Angel Alley
84b Whitechapel High Street,
London
E1 7QX
www.freedompress.org.uk
020 7247 9249

Green Books
Foxhole
Dartington
Totnes
Devon TQ9 6EB
www.greenbooks.co.uk
01803 863 260

Green Building Press
PO Box 32
Llandysul
Carmarthenshire
Wales SA44 5ZA
www.greenbuildingpress.co.uk
01559 370 798

Housmans Bookshop
5 Caledonian Road
Kings Cross
London N1 9DX
020 7837 4473

www.housmans.com
(Home of the Peace Diary, available every year)

Indymedia
www.indymedia.org.uk
imc-uk-
contact@lists.indymedia.org

Natterjack Press
PO BOX 74
Brighton BN1 4ZQ
www.natterjackpress.co.uk

News from Nowhere Bookshop
96 Bold Street
Liverpool L1 4HY
www.newsfromnowhere.org.uk
0151 708 7270

Schnews
c/o Community Base
113 Queens Road
Brighton BN1 3XG
www.schnews.org.uk
01273 685913

Word Power Bookshop
43-45 West Nicolson Street
Edinburgh EH8 9DB
www.word-power.co.uk
0131 662 9112

Labour, fair trade, anti-poverty and trade unions

Clean Clothes Campaign
Labour Behind the Label
10-12 Picton Street
Bristol BS6 5QA
www.cleanclothes.org
0117 944 1700

The Fairtrade Foundation
3rd Floor
Ibex House
42-47 Minories
London EC3N 1DY
www.fairtrade.org.uk
020 7405 5942

Labour Behind the Label
10-12 Picton Street
Bristol BS6 5QA
www.labourbehindthelabel.org
0117 944 1700

Living Wage Campaign
www.livingwagecampaign.org

No Sweat
5 Caledonian Road
London N1 9DX
www.nosweat.org.uk
07904 431 959

Oxfam
Oxfam House
John Smith Drive
Cowley
Oxford OX4 2JY
www.oxfam.org
01865 473 727

Railway Children
1st Floor
1 The Commons
Sandbach
Cheshire CW11 1EG
www.railwaychildren.org.uk
01270 757596

Trades Union Congress
Congress House
Great Russell Street
London WC1B 3LS
www.tuc.org.uk
0207 636 4030

Traidcraft
Kingsway
Gateshead
Tyne and Wear NE11 0NE
www.traidcraft.co.uk
0191 491 0591

Unite
Unite House
128 Theobald's Road
London WC1X 8TN
www.tgwu.org.uk
020 7611 2500

War on Want
Development House
56-64 Leonard Street
London EC2A 4LT
www.waronwant.org
020 7549 0555 or 0845 193
1952

Which?
Castlemead
Gascoyne Way
Hertford SG14 1LH
www.which.co.uk
01992 822800

**World Development
Movement**
66 Offley Road
London SW9 0LS
www.wdm.org.uk
0207 820 4900

Lawyers who specialise in environmental or human rights law

Bindmans
275 Gray's Inn Road
London WC1X 8QB
www.bindmans.com
020 7833 4433

Christian Khan
5 Gower Street
Bloomsbury
London WC1E 6HA
www.christiankhan.co.uk
020 7631 9500

Climate Justice
www.climatelaw.org
020 7388 3141

Earthjustice
www.earthjustice.org

EarthRights Solicitors
Springfield
Kilmington
Axminster
Devon EX13 7SB
www.earthrights.org.uk
01297 34405

Environmental Law Foundation
Suite 309
16 Baldwins Gardens
London EC1N 7RJ
www.elflaw.org
020 7404 1030

Hodge Jones and Allen
180 North Gower Street
London NW1 2NB
www.hja.net
0800 437 0080

Leigh Day & Co
Priory House
25 St John's Lane
London EC1M 4LB
www.leighday.co.uk
020 7650 1200

Peace and human rights

Aldermaston Women's Peace Camp
www.aldermaston.net
07969 739 812

Amnesty International UK
The Human Rights Action Centre
17-25 New Inn Yard
London EC2A 3EA
www.amnesty.org.uk
020 7033 1500

Block the Builders
www.blockthebuilders.org.uk

Campaign Against Arms Trade
11 Goodwin St
Finsbury
London N4 3HQ
www.caat.org.uk
0207 281 0297

Campaign for Nuclear Disarmament
Mordechai Vanunu House
162 Holloway Road
London N7 8DQ
www.cnduk.org
0207 700 2393

The Conscience Campaign
Archway Resource Centre
1b Waterlow Road
London N19 5NJ

www.conscienceonline.org.uk
020 7561 1061
Under this umbrella: Peace Tax
Seven www.peacetaxseven.com

Liberty
21 Tabard Street
London SE1 4LA
www.liberty-human-rights.org.uk
020 7403 3888

Peace Pledge Union
1 Peace Passage
London N7 0BT
www.ppu.org.uk
020 7424 9444

Rock Against Racism aka Love Music Hate Racism
PO Box 2566
London N4 1WJ
www.lovemusichateracism.com
020 7801 2781

Trident Ploughshares
42-46 Bethel St
Norwich NR2 1NR
www.tridentploughshares.org
0845 4588366

Voices in the Wilderness
www.vitw.org

Political parties and useful public offices

Conservative Party
Conservative Campaign
Headquarters
30 Millbank
London SW1P 4DP
www.conservatives.com
020 7222 9000

Co-operative Party
77 Weston Street
London SE1 3SD
www.party.coop
020 7367 4150

Electoral Commission
Trevelyan House
Great Peter Street
London SW1P 2HW
www.electoralcommission.org.uk
020 7271 0500

Equality and Human Rights
3 More London
Riverside Tooley Street
London SE1 2RG
www.equalityhumanrights.com
020 3117 0235

Cardiff
3rd floor, 3 Callaghan Square
Cardiff, CF10 5BT
02920 447710

Glasgow
The Optima Building
58 Robertson Street
Glasgow G2 8DU
0141 228 5910

European Commission in London
8 Storey's Gate
London SW1P 3AT
http://ec.europa.eu/united-kingdom

Fabian Society
11 Dartmouth Street
London SW1H 9BN
http://fabians.org.uk
020 7227 4900

Green Party
1A Waterlow Road
London N19 5NJ
www.greenparty.org.uk
020 7272 4474

Information Commissioner's Office

Information Commissioner's
Office – England
Wycliffe House
Water Lane
Wilmslow
Cheshire SK9 5AF
08456 30 60 60/01625 54 57 45

Information Commissioner's
Office – Scotland,
93-95 Hanover Street
Edinburgh EH2 1DJ
0131 301 5071

Information Commissioner's
Office – Wales,
Cambrian Buildings
Mount Stuart Square
Cardiff CF10 5FL
029 2044 8044

Information Commissioner's
Office - Northern Ireland,
51 Adelaide Street
Belfast BT2 8FE
028 9026 9380

Labour Party

39 Victoria Street
London SW1H 0HA
www.labour.org.uk
08705 900 200

Liberal Democrats

4 Cowley Street
London SW1P 3NB

www.libdems.org.uk
020 7222 7999

Local Government Association

Local Government House
Smith Square
London SW1P 3HZ
www.lga.gov.uk
020 7664 3131

Natural England

1 East Parade
Sheffield S1 2ET
www.naturalengland.org.uk
0845 6003078

New Philanthropy Capital

3 Downstream
1 London Bridge
London SE1 9BG
www.philanthropycapital.org
020 7785 6300

Socialist Workers Party

PO Box 42184
London SW8 2WD
www.swp.org.uk
020 7819 1170

They Work for You

www.theyworkforyou.com

Write to Them

www.writetothem.com

Privacy, democracy, rights

Fathers 4 Justice Ltd
PO Box 500
Winchester SO21 1AX
www.fathers-4-justice.org
office@fathers-4-justice.org

Howard League for Penal Reform
1 Ardleigh Road
London N1 4HS
www.howardleague.org
020 7249 7373

No2ID
Box 412
19-21 Crawford Street
London W1H 1P
www.no2id.net
07005 800 651

Privacy International
265 Strand
London
WC2R 1BH
www.privacyinternational.org
020 8123 7933

Unlock Democracy incorporating Charter 88
Basement
6 Cynthia Street
London N1 9JF
www.charter88.org.uk
020 7278 4443

Bibliography

Nick Wates and Christian Wolmar (eds), *Squatting: The Real Story*
Bay Leaf Books, 1980

Hannah Arendt, *On Revolution*
Penguin, 1990

Geoffrey Ashe, *The Offbeat Radicals: The British Tradition of Alternative Dissent*
Methuen, 2007

Ian Bone, Bash the Rich: True Life Confessions of an Anarchist in the UK
Tangent Books, 2006

Billy Bragg, *The Progressive Patriot: A Search for Belonging*
Black Swan, 2006

Asa Briggs, *The Age of Improvement*
Longman, 1975

Asa Briggs, *A Social History of England*
Penguin, 1986

Pam Brown, *Henry Dunant*
Exley Publications, 1988

Omar Cabezas, *Fire from the Mountain: The Making of a Sandinista*
Jonathan Cape, 1985

Noam Chomsky, "On Resistance", *The New York Review of Books*
December 7 1967

Stuart Christie, *Granny Made Me an Anarchist: General Franco, the Angry Brigade and Me*
Scribner, 2004

Matthew Collin, *The Time of the Rebels*
Serpent's Tail, 2007

Terry Collingsworth, *ATCA: A Vital Tool for Preventing Corporations from Violating Fundamental Human Rights* from www.laborrights.org

Chris Cook, *Britain in the Nineteenth Century, 1815–1914*
Routledge, 2005

George Dangerfield, *The Strange Death of Liberal England*
Paladin, 1970

Julie Ann Davies, "The Agents of Influence: MPs and Lobbying Companies". *Spinwatch,*
April 18 2006

Norman Davies, *Europe: A History*
Pimlico, 1996

Richard Dawkins, "Atheists for Jesus",
richarddawkins.net, April 11 2006

Martyn Day, *Environmental Action: A Citizen's Guide*
Pluto Press, 1998

Bernadette Dohrn, Bill Ayers and Jeff Jones, *Sing a Battle Song: The Revolutionary Poetry, Statements and Communiqués of the Weather Underground*
Seven Stories Press, 2006

Jonathan Drimmer, "Don't Be Dubbed a Human Rights Abuser",
Legal Times, October 22 2007

Daniel Ellsberg, Secrets: *A Memoir of Vietnam and the Pentagon Papers*
Penguin Books, 2002

Frederick Engels, *The Condition of the Working Classes in England in 1844*
George Allen and Unwin, 1950

Jacquie L'Etang, *Public Relations in Britain*
Routledge, 2004

Louis Fischer, *The Life of Mahatma Gandhi*
HarperCollins, 1997

Paul Foot, *The Vote: How It Was Won and How It Was Undermined*
Penguin, 2006

Yves Fremion, *Orgasms of History: 3,000 Years of Spontaneous Insurrection*
AK Press, 2002

Erich Fromm, *Escape from Freedom*
Owl Books, 1965

Arun Gandhi, *Daughter of Midnight: The Child Bride of Gandhi*
Blake Publishing, 1998

Peter Gelderloos, *How Nonviolence Protects the State*
Southend Press, 2007

Malcolm Gladwell, *The Tipping Point*
Abacus, 2000

AC Grayling, *Towards the Light: The Story of the Struggle for Liberty and Rights*
Bloomsbury, 2007

Jasper Griegson, *The Complete Complainer: How to Complain and Get Results*
Metro Books, 2000

Richard Gregg, "Moral Jiu-Jitsu", in *Nonviolent Direct Action*, eds A Paul Hare and Herbert H Blumberg, 1968

Che Guevara, *Guerilla Warfare*
Souvenir Press, 2004

Peter Hain, *Don't Play with Apartheid: The Background to the Stop the Seventy Campaign*
Allen and Unwin, 1971

WD Handcock, *English Historical Documents 1874–1914*
Routledge, 1996

A Paul Hare and Herbert H Blumberg (eds), *Nonviolent Direct Action, American Cases: Social Psychological Analyses*
Corpus Publications, 1968

Tim Harford, *The Undercover Economist*
Abacus, 2006

Chris Harman, *Revolution in the 21st Century*
Bookmarks, 2007

Archibald Henderson, *George Bernard Shaw*
Kessinger Publishing, 2004

Christopher Hill, *The World Turned Upside Down: Radical Ideas during the English Revolution*
Penguin, 1975

Thomas Hobbes, *Leviathan*
Penguin, 1968

Tristram Hunt, *The English Civil War at First Hand*
Weidenfeld & Nicolson, 2002

Robert Hunter, *The Greenpeace Chronicle*
Picador, 1979

Lewis Hyde, *The Gift*
Canongate, 2007

Claborne Carson, *Martin Luther King, The Autobiography*
Abacus, 2007

Charles Kingsley, *The Water Babies*
Wordsworth Editions, 1994

Mark Kurlansky, *Non-violence: The History of a Dangerous Idea*
Jonathan Cape, 2006

Tim Lang and Yiannis Gabriel, "A Brief History of Consumer Activism" in *The Ethical Consumer*, eds Rob Harrison, Terry Newholm, Deirdre Shaw
Sage Publications, 2005

Daniel Leader, *Business and Human Rights: Time to Hold Companies to Account*
Speech, 2007

Shevawn Lynam, *Humanity Dick*
Hamish Hamilton, 1975

FSL Lyons, *Ireland Since the Famine*
Fontana Press, 1985

Brian MacArthur, *The Penguin Book of Twentieth Century Protest*
Viking Books, 1998

Niccolo Machiavelli, *The Prince*
Penguin, 2003

Keith Mann, *From Dusk Till Dawn: An Insider's View of the Growth of the Animal Liberation Movement*
Puppy Pincher Press, 2007

Peter Marshall, *Demanding the Impossible: A History of Anarchism*
Fontana Press, 1993

Karl Marx, *Capital*
Oxford University Press, 2000

John Stuart Mill and Jeremy Bentham, *Utilitarianism and Other Essays*
Penguin, 2004

George Monbiot, *The Age of Consent: A Manifesto For a New World Order*
Harper Collins, 2003

Kenneth O Morgan, *Labour People: Hardie to Kinnock*
Oxford University Press, 1987

David Ogilvy, *Ogilvy on Advertising*
Pan, 2007

Massimo de Angelis, Starhawk, Antonio Negri and others,
On Fire: The Battle of Genoa and the Anti-Capitalist Movement
One Off Press, 2001

RJ Overy, *The Inter-War Crisis 1919–1939*
Pearson Education, 1994

Thomas Paine, *The Rights of Man*
Dover Publications, 1999

Melanie Phillips, *The Ascent of Woman: A History of the Suffragette Movement
and the Ideas Behind It*
Abacus, 2003

Frances Fox Piven and Richard A Cloward, *Poor People's Movements:
Why They Succeed, How They Fail*
First Vintage Books, 1979

David Powell and Tom Hickey (eds), *Democracy, the Long Revolution*
Continuum Books, 2007

Patricia Pugh, Educate, Agitate, *Organise: 100 years of Fabian Socialism*
Methuen and Co, 1984

Diane Purkiss, *The English Civil War: A People's History*
Harper Collins, 2006

Matt Ridley, *The Origins of Virtue*
Penguin Books, 1996

Geoffrey Robertson, *Crimes Against Humanity: The Struggle for Global Justice*
Penguin, 2006

Jean-Jacques Rousseau, *The Social Contract*
Penguin, 1968

EF Schumacher, *Small Is Beautiful: A Study of Economics as if People Mattered*
Abacus, 1973

GR Searle, *A New England: Peace and War, 1886–1918*
Clarendon Press, 2004

Mark Steel, *Reasons to Be Cheerful*
Scribner, 2001

James Surowiecki, *The Wisdom of Crowds: Why the Many are Smarter than the Few*
Abacus, 2004

Mark Thomas, *As Used on the Famous Nelson Mandela*
Random House, 2006

EP Thompson, *The Making of the English Working Class*
Penguin, 1980

Henry David Thoreau, *Civil Disobedience and Other Essays*
Dover Publications, 1993

Leo Tolstoy, *The Kingdom of God Is Within You.*
Cassell Publishing Company, 1894, www.nonresistance.org, 2004

Trapese Collective, *Do It Yourself: A Handbook for Changing Our World*
Pluto Press, 2007

Robert Tressell, *The Ragged-Trousered Philanthropists*
Penguin, 2004

John Vidal, *McLibel: Burger Culture on Trial*
Macmillan, 1997

PAJ Waddington, "Policing Public Order and Political Contention",
in *A Handbook of Policing*, ed Tim Newburn.
Willan Publishing, 2003

Francis Wheen, *Karl Marx*
Fourth Estate, 2000

Which? 50 years, 1957–2007, October 2007

AN Wilson, *The Victorians*
Arrow Books, 2002

Ben Wilson, *The Laughter of Triumph: William Hone and the Fight for the
Free Press*
Faber and Faber, 2005

Robert Wright, *The Moral Animal: Why We Are the Way We Are*
Abacus, 1994

Index

ALSO PUBLISHED BY GUARDIAN BOOKS

A WORLD WITHOUT BEES

Alison Benjamin and Brian McCallum

The western honeybee plays a vital role within the planet's cco-system, pollinating 70 per cent of the food that we eat. Yet the future of the honeybee is under threat, and the rate at which their numbers continue to diminish, has led to fears that we are dangerously out of sync with nature.

A World Without Bees charts the fascinating history of the western honeybee and investigates the reasons for their rapid decline in numbers. This inspiring account will cause its readers to face the potential consequences of the honeybees' fragile existence, and cause them to look into the personal actions that can be taken to ensurc their future survival.

'A timely and important exploration of the crucial role bees play in all our lives and the deadly threats they are facing.'
Vince Cable, beekeeper and politician

'Benjamin and McCallum have trawled through a vast well of knowledge on bees, founded on millennia of observation and experimentation, and the result is a thoroughly readable book.'
Jonathan Jones, BBC Wildlife Magazine

'A highly enjoyable, polished, well-researched homage to the honeybee.'
Observer

'The success of A World Without Bees lies in its explanation of the challenges faced by the honeybee population and the intensiveness of commercial beekeeping.'
Daily Telegraph

ISBN: 978-0852651315

RRP: £7.99

WILD SWIM

River, Lake, Lido and Sea:
The Best Places to Swim Outdoors in Britain

Kate Rew with photographs by Dominick Tyler

In this stunning, full-colour guide, Kate Rew, founder
of the Outdoor Swimming Society, takes the reader on a
wild journey through Britain, covering 200 rivers, lakes,
tidal pools, lidos, estuaries and sea swims.

Whether you are a seasoned outdoor swimmer looking to
discover a hidden fairy pool, or a young family seeking a fun day
out, Wild Swim has all the information and inspiration you'll
need to get you stripping and dipping.

'... like a glossy recipe book, only with pictures of delicious lakes and rivers
where you would normally find soufflés and stews, and mouth-watering
descriptions in lochs and oceans instead of recipes...'
Craig Brown, Mail on Sunday Book of the Week

'A practical guide to pools and beauty spots combined with imagery that perfectly
captures the freshness and freedom of elemental swimming.'
Charlotte Ross, Evening Standard

'Will have you hunched on the sofa as though with a stash of love letters.'
Antonia Quirke, New Statesman

'Packed with elegiac photography of boys on rope swings, laughter, swimmers in
reeds and algae-green ponds that will sustain you all the way into the water, past
the toe-dipping point of no return.' Matt Rudd, Sunday Times

'Covering swims from the Hebrides to Cornwall, this is also a guide to great
places to pitch up for the day – usually at an easy distance from a good, steamy-
windowed café.' Good Housekeeping

ISBN: 978-0852651223

RRP: £12.99

MONEY BACK GUARANTEED

Anna Tims

When was the last time you thought you deserved
a refund? Or wanted to complain about the service you were
getting? And did you actually get the result you wanted?

Every day hundreds of legitimate complaints get
lost in a mess of corporate bureaucracy, outsourced
departments and labyrinthine procedures. We're often
left frustrated when our voices aren't heard, having
to resign ourselves to substandard service.

Not any more. Anna Tims has been championing
consumer rights in the *Guardian* for 10 years and with her
book you can finally redress the balance. Covering everything
from insurance providers to internet services, and from travel
agents to utility companies, this book shows you how and when
things can go wrong, provides strategies to help you arm
yourself against disaster and most importantly
gives advice on getting things put right.

When times are tough and every penny counts,
Money Back Guaranteed is your ticket to regaining control.
Because if you know who to complain to, when to
broach the subject and how to get attention, chances
are you will achieve your goal.

ISBN: 978-0852651469

RRP: £7.99